ELUSIVE DREAM

ELUSIVE DREAM

Mickey's Elusive Dream

Alan Neil

ELUSIVE DREAM
MICKEY'S ELUSIVE DREAM

iUniverse books may be ordered through booksellers or by contacting:

iUniverse
1663 Liberty Drive
Bloomington, IN 47403
www.iuniverse.com
1-800-Authors (1-800-288-4677)

ISBN: 978-1-5320-5792-2 (sc)
ISBN: 978-1-5320-5793-9 (e)

Library of Congress Control Number: 2018911036

Print information available on the last page.

iUniverse rev. date: 10/04/2018

MICKEY G (MY FRIEND)

Mickey G was my friend. This is a story about his father. Mickey grew up without his father and he was in his late 50's before he learned what happened to his father and why his father never returned home. I feel very lucky that my life and Mickeys crossed paths.

It was in 1983 that I first met Mickey and for no apparent reason he seemed to hate me and everything about me. We were working together in Kuwait and the war between Iraq and Iran was going strong. The nightly shows of artillery duels along the Faw Peninsula were a regular occurrence but even though the war was close it didn't seem like much of a war and no one was winning. Some days we saw dog fights between the Russian Mig airplanes belonging to Iraq and the old F4 Phantoms American made and being flown by Iran. When the loser ran out of bullets they seemed to use the Kuwait airport as an escape route and would head back to their respective bases to make new plans. America had stopped selling Iran bullets and bombs for their planes so the dog fights slowed down but the artillery duels become colorful just after sundown. The Iran revolutionary guard was not a match for Iraq but they were persistent in attacking the Faw peninsula where the great rivers the Tigress and the Euphrates entered the Arabian Gulf. The Iraq army and their advantage of prevailing winds made the use of nerve gas, mustard gas and chlorine gas to keep the

Faw peninsula and their ability to export oil. All of this ended when the winds shifted and the Iraq army gassed themselves. The Iranians army walked in afterwards and took over and got stronger in controlling the rivers access to the Gulf, the dead bodies were fed to the fish and when the local fish markets started finding dead soldier body parts inside of fish the war became serious and disgusting.

Kuwait had a marketing plan to extract more profit for their oil. They were building a new refinery and expanding capacity in their old one. In the future they would sell more refined products. Mickey and I were helping them. Mickey was a general superintendent for construction and I worked in Project Management. My job was to make sure construction was fed with timely materials and manpower to install and build. Mickey's job was to build 450,000 barrels per day refinery and upgrade the existing refinery to 150,000 barrels per day capacity. We had reasons to talk every day but we couldn't find a reason to like each other and somehow the mention of Texas, my birthplace, seemed to be a real burr under Mickey's saddle. Mickey was raised in Northern California but had worked in many places. We shared some of our experiences at our breakfast, lunch and supper table where 10 of us ate every meal together. It turned out that 3 of us had played professional baseball. Mickey was drafted by the LA Dodgers and played in their lower divisions of minor league ball, Frank a member of our table also played for the dodgers. Mickey was a second baseman and Frank was a pitcher. I cut my thumb off when I was 16 with a possibility of being drafted ended but I managed to play money ball for several years. Baseball was the only conversation we could enjoy without being offensive.

Mickey life had many interesting parts, had idolized the old mobsters that lived and operated around Reno. California near the where he grew up. They helped him with the trade unions in his early employment. Most interesting was his friendship with the controversial comedian Lenny Bruce. Lenny found humor and sarcasm with his views on the hypocrisy of government operations and their Mob connections. Mickey had been Lennie's roommate and friend. Lenny's life and death was controvoisal and every bit as mysterious as Marylyn Monroe's. The government killed Lenny and his death helped Mickey start a long career working overseas.

Mickey never spoke of having children or being married several times but when questioned about how he opened his mail provided some insight. In the days before email receiving a letter was usually a big deal and the mail was given out before the weekly staff meeting. Mickey had ruled that no one be allowed to open their mail until the meeting had concluded. When Mickey opened his own mail he took a small knife and cut open the letter from the bottom seam. If the letter was from someone that he didn't want to acknowledge, he would read, reinsert in the envelope, tape the cut together and write "not known at this address" and "Return to Sender". He would sign PM for post master. Usually he would comment something about "dam lawyers as he gave a big smile"

Mickey never spoke about his family. He entertained the breakfast, lunch and supper club with his wit and humor. No one was spared except me. His comments to me were usually vindictive except about work or baseball. I really didn't understood until the day I ask him why he hated me. Mickey told me his father was a Texan and had abandoned his family who were forced to survive by their own skills. He never understood how any man could do that. My first memory of him hating me was the day the club was discussing what job they wanted to do when they grew up. Baseball was at the top of the list but when I said that I wanted to be a cowboy and work on the King Ranch in Texas; Mickey looked at me with contempt and got up and walked away without speaking. I never again spoke about wanting to be a cowboy.

A member of our club was the company lawyer named Charlie. Mickey loved to verbally spar with Charlie who was recently divorced. Charlie was a born and bred California lawyer. One day he told me that he wanted me to join him in a secret meeting with some Kuwaitis and warned me to "not go cowboy in the meeting" Mickey had a smile as wide as Texas that seemed to say to Charlie "Don't worry, he will be fine"

At the secret meeting we discussed a Kuwaiti contractor who had been a pain in my ass for making slow and unreliable deliveries. Their business manager and I had some disputes. Their BM was an upper caste Indian who always acted like he could do no wrong and I was being unreasonable. I had withdrawn some of his orders and gave them to his competition from Qatar. Qatar had just built a large steel plant and prices were very competitive. The BM was upset but his steel was coming from India and the Indian steel business was on hard times because the Chinese were kicking their butts. In the meeting I provided proof that promised deliveries and prices were not being met. I also stated that I was responsible for the money I was spending even though it belonged to Kuwait, I thought they had trusted me as I would trust someone and I would do my best for their good. One of the Kuwaitis stood up and says "this meeting is over, Neil please join me outside there is something I want to tell you." We walked outside the old abandoned building where the meeting was held and out of view of the others. The man grabbed me, hugged me, and told me "I am so proud of you because I am the person responsible for all of Kuwait's money. My family has always been responsible for Kuwait's money, I am the Finance Minister but my family started Kuwait and no one wanted to be King. I will make sure your prices are honored and your deliveries are met. My family started by making ships, you have visited the original factory and have seen how Kuwait was build. I respect your values and understand your temperament but I want you to try and be nicer to people" When the conversation ended with another hug we both had tears in our eyes. I would think of this man as Iraq invaded Kuwait and most Kuwaitis ran to Europe like scared dogs but this man relocated to Egypt and continued his work as Finance Minister. I would also think about Mickey smiling for me mixed with his razor cutting eyes at Charlie when he told me "Don't go cowboy in this meeting" Mickey knew I didn't need to go anywhere to be a cowboy but I had no idea that Mickey's father was a real cowboy who had worked on the King Ranch in Texas.

Years later Mickey called me and invited me to lunch. He also invited Mike a protégé of himself. Mickey had mentored and trained Mike throughout his career so I agreed and we met for lunch for at a steak house on Houston's Southwest freeway. The restaurant was located near an overpass. Mickey looked strange because half of his jaw had been removed during his battle with bone cancer. When asked if we wanted to sit in smoking or non-smoking I said "It really doesn't matter because Mickey already had cancer. Mike looked appalled but Mickey laughed and his eyes light up. We were seated and Mickey gave us an update on his struggle. He was still consulting for friends and busy in spite of his cancer fight. He said he had fought hard but was losing the battle and he was ending treatment. I was shocked and uncontrollable tears ran down my cheeks. Mike was shocked and the look on his face was exactly like the look on my little brother's face when our mother passed. He spoke to Mike first and told him to arrange his funeral and tell his friends that he fought hard but had lost. Then he handed me this book and told me to publish it. He said "It may help some kid who grew up without a father". I recalled the day in Kuwait when Mickey came running into my office and told me they have found my father. Without looking up I said "Was he black" Then Mickey cursed me out and ran to tell Mike. Later that day he told me his father was in Alaska scouting places to start a beef ranch to provide food for Americans fighting in the Pacific during world war two. His plane crashed on a mountain on Kodiak Island but no one knew what happened until the airplane was discovered years later and the search party found a Rolex watch with the engraving "Jack Gotcher". Mickey's father had been found after 46 years.

As we left the restaurant a car accident happened on the wet interstate and one car was half way over the bridges guard rail directly above us. I imagined another car hitting the hanging car and falling on the three of us. I was looking and thinking about a safe place to run to before we all were killed. As I looked for safety Mickey screamed "We have to get up on that bridge and help them". He was livid about helping the women in the car. Mike and I could have climbed the 30 or 40 feet but there were too much fast traffic and an unstable car hanging over the guard rail. I heard sirens and knew help was on the way in just a few minutes so I told Mickey to wait. It happened fast but a fire truck pulled the car off the rail and the women were safe in minutes I am still amazed by Mickey's reactions just days before his death.

This is his story and it deserves to be told as requested by my Friend Mickey G. RIP Mickey

THE ELUSIVE RAINBOW

THE JACK GOTCHER STORY

CHAPTER 1

THE EARLY YEARS

My mom, Lona Porterfield, was born in Cisco, Texas, Eastland County, which is located near the true center of Texas. The year was 1882. The following year, a devastating tornado leveled the town of Cisco, killing 28 residents and leaving nearly all the remaining people homeless. Her family, the John Porterfields, lost their home without loss of life or limb. They relocated to the nearby community of Rising Star.

Very early in life, my mom became a deeply devoted religious person. She was a sweet God-fearing, God-loving person throughout life. She met my father, James T. Gotcher, at a revival in Rising Star in the fall of 1897 and they married two weeks later. Dad was 21 and Mom was 15 and a half.

James was a ranch hand, sometimes cowboy and other times a trader of horses, sheep, or whatever he could buy and sell later at a profit. He was attending the revival as other young cowboys did in that day. "To show their respect to the Lord and to meet the young ladies."

The marriage did not last much longer than it took to consummate it. James's lust for the life of a cowboy and his desire to return to his birthplace of Lampasas, Texas, overcame the vows of marriage. He was gone within two weeks and did not know for a couple of years that Lona had become pregnant during this brief period. She had given birth to me, Reuben Everett Gotcher, on June 10th, 1898.

Though both mom and dad communicated enough to get an annulment, she did not tell him about the pregnancy or my birth. Ironically, both remarried less than a year after their original marriage. Each had a child by a new mate in late 1899.

I was about a year and a half old when my brother, Horace Odum (later known as Skinny), was born. Two years later, a sister, Jan, was born.

Charlie Pollack, the name my stepfather answered to, tried to do a little farming and any general handyman work that he could. Mom raised a few chickens and rabbits and we had eggs, rabbit, and occasionally some lamb as our main staples. There was never any extra money. If there was, it was given to the church. However, as a four year old, I thought we were doing well, although it seemed that mom and Charlie were doing a lot of arguing.

Mom mentioned to me that I needed to go see my real father. This scared me to death as I had never seen the man and it hadn't been very long ago that she let him, or me, know of each other.

When not taking care of family, mom attended every church event that came up. If there was a revival in town, she would attend all seven nights and, if it was within 20 miles, she would make it as often as she could get a ride.

Charlie kept insisting to mom that we just could not continue feeding five mouths and that I would have to go. Women in that era always seemed to let the man have the final word.

Though I knew something was going to happen, I was still surprised when one morning my mom and stepfather woke me early. Mom was crying as she folded the few clothes I had and tied them into an oversized bandana. This was tied to a bamboo pole. I still wasn't sure just what was going on.

We ate breakfast and, during the meal, my mom said, "Reuben, we are going to send you to see your father for a while. He is anxious to visit with you, but as soon as Charlie and I save a little money, we will want you to come back. Remember how much your mom loves you and will always love you." She then pinned a note on my shirt which read: "Please see that my boy gets to his father, James T. Gotcher, in Lampasas. Thank You."

At the south end of town, there were several dirt roads that crossed the stage lines and wagons hauling goods passed by here. Though there were railroads in many towns at this time, most of them were strictly from one town to another and one would have to change trains or take a stagecoach to the next place. We would not have had the money to put me on a train, so the availability was not looked into. I would be more or less hitchhiking to get a free ride.

My mom needed to get back to the house, as Horace and Jan had been left sleeping. We hugged and kissed and they turned and walked away. Ode showed no emotion, but mom and I sobbed quite loudly. I was four years old and not really ready for this.

The sun was rising and it was going to be a very hot day. It seemed like ages, but was only about 30 minutes before a wagon stopped. The teamster, who was hauling goods to Brownwood, asked where I was going and I pointed to the note pinned on my shirt. He read and said, "Come on, boy. I will take you to Brownwood and it will be easier from there."

It took us about five hours to reach Brownwood. Brownwood was the county seat of Brown County and had a population of almost 3,000. I had never seen such a big city. Of course, the only places I had been to were Cisco and Rising Star. Brownwood was the buying center for both wool and oil and, even on a weekday, there were several auctions going on.

The teamster told me to watch his goods and the wagon and he would try to find me a ride. He was gone almost two hours before he returned and said, "I've found you a ride as far as Scallorn, but it is not until early tomorrow morning. The people said that they would be by about 4:30 in the morning. Let's go get a bite to eat and you can sleep in the livery stable tonight. We went to the diner and I had one of my favorite meals: a bowl of beans, cornbread, and a glass of milk.

After eating, we walked back to the livery stable and he changed horses and headed out to Comanche. By then it must have been 4:00 p.m. and I hadn't had my usual afternoon nap. I went inside the stable, found a bale of hay in a corner, and cried myself to sleep. Despite my thoughts of the great adventure ahead, I missed my mom already. She was only 28 miles away and I could not understand why I couldn't be with her.

I heard voices in the stable and it was still very dark, but a man in his 30's said, "Are you the lad going to Scallorn?" I showed him the note and he told me to climb on the wagon. His wife was a heavy set woman and complained about everything. Not a word was said to me on the trip. I engaged my thoughts into things, like if my dad was rich. I wondered if he would buy a book so I could learn to read. I hoped that my stepmother would be nice, but was worried because most stores in that era were of the wicked stepmother. I also wondered if I would get some new clothes and a hat.

Scallorn was about 50 miles southeast of Brownwood and it took us from 4:30 a.m. until 1:00 p.m. to get there. I had nothing to eat on the trip. The people I was traveling with ate some sandwiches about 10:00 a.m., but ignored me in the back of the wagon.

The town of Scallorn was the opposite of Brownwood. It was the smallest town I had ever seen. There were six or seven houses, a church, a store, and a livery stable. It also had a small railroad house. The Gulf, Colorado, and Santa Fe railroads used it as a shipping and switching center. It had a turntable for engines like nothing I had ever seen. It was neat for such a little town.

The people told me to get down off the wagon and wished me well. I had no idea as to what to do or where to go. I spotted the livery stable and went there. I soon was asleep and slept until almost 5:00 p.m., when the owner of the stable came in and asked what I was doing. I showed him the note which was still on my shirt.

He kindly said, "Come with me, Son. My wife will fix us dinner and we'll make you a pallet to sleep on. I am sure I can find you a ride in the morning.

After a good dinner, I was required to take a bath and to wear the other set of clothes in my bandana. The wife of the stable owner washed my jeans and hung them on the clothesline to dry.

They told me that at 7:00 p.m., we would be going to the church that was a two room building located across the street from the livery stable. It was two houses away. My benefactors had a daughter who also attended church with us. I think she was about eleven. While the services started with a hymn and a prayer, I prayed for my mom and my family. I pictured mom being in church at the same time and praying for me. It seemed such a long time since I had seen them. It was already a day and a half.

Following the first prayer, the young people were told to go to the basement for young people's services. There were seven kids in all and no adults came down. The stable owner's daughter took charge and we were told the story of Joseph. I know that she must have told it quite often, as she seldom looked into the book. Following the services, the adults had coffee and we children were allowed to play hide and seek in the church yard. It was one of the few times I had gotten to play with a group of kids and I had a very good time. I sure slept well that night.

When I got up in the morning, I was given a breakfast of bacon, eggs, grits, and a big glass of milk. The lady folded my freshly washed clothes, tied them into the bandana, and put a jelly sandwich in with them. I would have lunch that day. She told me that her husband was at the stable and I should probably go on down there to see him. I thanked her and hugged her hips. She said, "Son, if you ever come through here again, be sure to stop and visit with us. We always have room for one more, and Jake and I would love to have a son." I believe she had a tear in her eye. They were really good people.

I walked to the stable and was greeted by the owner. He told me that he had found some people going to Lampasas. They knew my father and would be passing right by his place. After a short wait, a wagon pulled up and an elderly couple welcomed me aboard. After a few polite greetings, little more was said during the 30-mile trip. Around noon, they offered me some cold fried chicken that they had in a basket. I told them that I had a sandwich. We ate as the team of horses pulled us along.

Sometime around 3:00 in the afternoon, the old man stopped the wagon and pointed to a cabin which was about 150 yards from the trail. The driver said to me, "That's your dad's place. Tell him that Jess Cantwell says hello." I thanked them and jumped off the wagon.

Feeling a little scared, I started walking towards the cabin. About halfway there, my stepmother, Lillie, saw me and came toward me. She gave me a big hug and said, "So, you are Reuben. You must be hungry and tired. Why don't we clean you up? Your dad will be here in a couple of hours and will be anxious to see you. He is very excited about you coming to live with us."

The house had two rooms and a loft. One room had a kitchen and living area, the other was a bedroom. There were bunk beds against one wall in the living room. There were two young boys sleeping in the lower bunk. Miss Lillie told me that they were my brothers. Russell, age 3, and Lester, age 1. This was the first I knew that I had two more brothers. Dad must have remarried about the same time mom did.

Miss Lillie carried in several buckets of water from the well to fill a galvanized tub with water. I took a quick bath and was given cookies and milk. Miss Lillie told me I could sleep in the upper bunk or climb up to the loft and sleep on a pallet up there. I climbed onto the upper bunk and quickly fell asleep. I was feeling comfortable and was no longer scared.

Just before dark, a man with a heavy mustache and a big smile picked me out of the upper bunk. He gave me a hug and then said,

"Boy, what do they call you?" I responded with my given name, "Reuben, Sir." Dad looked at me with a smile and said, "Who would give a boy a name like that? From now on, you are Jack." And Jack I became for the reminder of my life. It made me very happy.

"When were you born Jack?" I held up four fingers, but he quickly said to me, "You will miss your birthday party if you don't know when it is." He worked with me and, by the end of the evening I was saying, "June 10th, 1898." I was a little disappointed when he told me that it had already passed and it would be next year before I had another one.

Miss Lillie was cooking dinner and all of dad's attention was being directed towards me. My younger brother, Russell, was getting jealous. He refused to let me sit on father's lap and started standing in a line between my dad and me. Les, who could barely walk, hung around Miss Lillie in the kitchen.

Dad asked, "Would you like to go to work with me tomorrow?" I nodded my head and said, "Yes, Sir." He said, "Well, I have to plow a field for the Andrews. You will need to keep the water in the shade and wipe down the horses when I stop to rest. Do you think you can handle that?" Again, I said, "Yes, Sir."

Miss Lillie said that dinner was ready, so we moved to the kitchen area. Cooking was done on a wood stove. There was a wooden table with two chairs and a small, elevated bench. Dinner was great: beef steak, potatoes, gravy, and cornbread.

During the meal, my father said to Miss Lillie, "The boy's name is Jack and that is what we will call him from now on. Now, what are we going to have him call you?" She replied, "He called me Miss Lillie when we first met and I guess he can call me that or mom." Father asked what I thought and I said, "Miss Lillie." And so that was agreed upon. I would never feel right about calling someone, other than my real mother, mom.

A bit later, dad told Miss Lillie to either write a letter to my mom or leave a note to be forwarded at the livery stable in Lampasas to let my mother know I had arrived safely. She said, "It might be better just to post a note at the livery stable, as it would cost a penny to mail it and it might take two weeks to be delivered."

Dad and I worked at various farms. We did plowing, planting, or whatever was needed. My main responsibilities were to wipe down the horses when they stopped, keep the water in the shade, and see that ants did not get to our lunches. A couple of times, I didn't take care of the water or the food properly. My father let me know, without raising his voice or making a threat that this was going to happen. I listened well.

Beside the work for others, we had about 15 fenced acres on which Miss Lillie raised a garden. We also had chickens, rabbits, a few turkeys, and some of the meanest geese you ever saw. One of my chores was feeding them and gathering eggs. The geese would see me coming and would attack with vengeance. They could get about three feet off the ground, flapping wings and kicking their feet. The turkeys did the same in a lesser degree. I soon learned to try to sneak the food out there while they were in a different part of the pen, dump the food, and run. This worked sometimes. I believe that my stepmother and my father were often watching and laughing in the house.

We often had a few lambs in the back. Dad would pick them up at the auction, fatten them up, and sell them at a profit. Occasionally, he would buy a sick lamb and try to get it on its feet to where it was salable. If it lived, there would be a good profit. If it died, it could be used for dog food. We always had three or four dogs of mixed breeds around.

On Thursdays, I generally stayed indoors and helped entertain Russell and Lester while Miss Lillie took care of laundry and other household necessities.

Lampasas was a nice sized community with about 1,500 residents. It was located on the Sulphur Fork of the Lampasas River. It was a railroad junction used for shipping wool, hides, and cotton.

On Saturdays, it was a family thing to get up early, hook up the buggy, and make the trip into town. Dad would usually ride along beside us on his horse. This way, he could do the things he needed to do without saddling the rest of us to hang around all day. He would start off at the auction looking for early bargains on anything, then go to the barber shop and livery stable to see what all was going on. Miss Lillie would take us to the general store and purchase the household necessities and usually a piece of candy for my brothers and me. We would then return home, with or without father.

I often marveled at my father's ability to recognize things that were a good deal and sell them at a profit. Often at the auction, he would buy a calf or a lamb, a plow, a saddle, or other farming equipment. He would tell Miss Lillie that we would have to remain in town a little longer. He wanted to load it on the wagon and put a "For Sale" sign on it and park it by the general store. I don't know how he knew, but he usually turned a profit in very short order. Sometimes the same item would be available at the auction and could have been had for less than he was charging for it, but they would buy from him. Of course, some people are very shy about bidding. Also, I think most knew that my dad had inspected it and would stand behind it. He had a good reputation in the community and was well liked.

Messages were posted at the general store and Miss Lillie spent time reading all of them. Thinking back, it was probably like reading someone else's mail, but there was always the chance that one would be for the Gotcher family. We were particularly watching for one from my mom. We wanted to be sure she knew that I had arrived in Lampasas. It was almost three months before a note from her was posted. It said that things were well there and she missed me and was glad I had made the trip safely. Miss Lillie said she would write one back to her for me. It would be posted on our next trip to town.

My mom mentioned that Charles had been called away and she doubted if she would ever marry again. About a month later, we got a message that she had married a man names Otis Odum.

Things remained calm and quiet at home. A lot of men dropped by the house to visit with my dad and they would talk about livestock

9

and farming. I was now five and a half and dad let me hitch up the horses. I could ride his horse. He had brought two mules for plowing, but they were a little too stubborn for me to handle. I spent many hours riding his horse and would hang on while he was trotting pretty fast. He taught me how to soap the tack and keep all the gear in good shape.

Father and I had gotten closer and closer all the time. I sure missed my mom still, but was fortunate that dad was getting to be a close second. Miss Lillie was certainly a great stepmother. One day while we were working a field, he came over by me and sat down for a drink of water. He said, "Jack, one of the things I have missed in life is that I never learned to read or write. I think that you should take advantage of any chance to learn these things, if possible. I am not going to force you to go to school, but if you would like to go, I think that maybe I can arrange it. Give it some thought and we will see what can be done." I didn't need to give it any thought. I said, "That is really something I want to do, Dad." He said that he would see what could be done. I was really excited. Pretty soon I would be able to write a letter to my mother.

That evening, Miss Lillie was told that Russell and I would be starting school whenever we could. He directed her to find out how we would go about getting in. She seemed as excited as Russell and me. She told dad that we would need some new clothes, boots, shirts, and jeans. He said, "One thing at a time. Buy one item per week." She did as told and we slowly acquired a wardrobe.

By the time school started, we both had a book and a few new items of clothing. Though it was almost two miles to the schoolhouse, our parents felt that we were responsible enough to go it alone. The excitement of the first few days had us running back and forth. In a month or two, we were doing some fooling around and were tardy a couple of times. The teacher set us straight by sending a note home to our parents. Dad had already talked to us about getting home to do chores and no more warnings were given.

This time, we made the dreaded trip to the woodshed. I believe that was the only time he ever spanked me.

I really enjoyed school and our teacher. Miss Reagan was really nice. The school had one room and there were 22 kids in grades 1 through 10. A 10th grade education at that time was considered almost the same as a college degree. In slightly over a year, I passed the second grade and was all geared up to go on to the third grade.

In May of 1905, about the same time that school was letting out for summer vacation, a letter arrived from my mom. She and Odie were doing well. There had been an addition to the family. A boy named Fletcher was a little over a year old and another child was on its way. Mom said things were pretty good and they had a little money saved. She said that if I could come home, she would send a ticket for me to ride the stage back.

I was now torn between two homes. I had grown to love my dad, my brothers, and Miss Lillie. I hadn't seen my mom in almost three years and she was the first love of my life. Dad was great. He knew where my heart was and consented for me to go.

He did have a long discussion with me. I recall him saying that people bring a lot of hardships on themselves and he was afraid that my mom might be one of those. Telling me that he did not want me to have to go through that type of life, he said if things started going bad to get back down to him and Miss Lillie. He said he had no idea what kind of a man my new stepfather was and that I should never allow anyone to mistreat me. On the day of my departure, we all had tears in our eyes. Russell, not understanding what I had gone through over the years, cried and begged them to let him go with me.

The stage pulled into town, changed the team of horses at the livery stable, and then went to the general store to pick up passengers. We said goodbye, she more tears, and the stage pulled out. I knew that I would miss them. They had been very good to me.

CHAPTER 2

HOME AGAIN

The buggy was built for speed, unlike the wagons I had traveled to Lampasas on. It had spring shocks on the wheels which kept you bouncing, making the ride feel as if it were a little softer than it they weren't there. We changed teams four times in the 80-mile trip to Brownwood. I would have like to have stayed overnight in Brownwood, as the last stage for Rising Star left at 2:30 p.m.

I did wander around Brownwood a bit, hoping to find a ride home that evening, but no luck. My butt was so sore from the bouncing on the buggy that I might not have been able to sit anyway.

I had my usual Brownwood favorite meal consisting of beans, cornbread, and milk. It cost fifteen cents, so I still had a dime left from the quarter my dad had given to me.

Before I bedded down in the stable, I met the man who would be driving the buggy to Rising Star the next morning. He told me I could ride on top with him. This was a special thrill. I could pretend I was riding shotgun.

Morning came and we left Brownwood at 8:00 a.m. We arrived in Rising Star about three hours later. All of the family was there to meet us except for Odie who was working.

We hugged, cried, and hugged some more. Horace remembered me and Jan acted like she did. Fletch had never seen me, but I was his big brother and he showed emotion.

We went back home and realized how crowded we were going to be. There was no loft like the one in my real dad's house. However, the storm cellar was under the house and it was only being used for storing jars of fruit my mom was canning and for keeping perishables fresh. I don't know how you would get a kid to stay down there alone, but at times, Horace and I tried it.

I met Odie that evening. He seemed like a nice man. He was the town handyman and had a knack for fixing automobiles. Cars were getting to be the rage. In the past five years, there had been a lot of oil discoveries in Texas. Cheap fuel, and the making of inexpensive vehicles by Henry Ford, was beginning to motorize America. There were now half a dozen automobiles in Rising Star alone.

I made a mistake at the dinner table by bragging that I could now read and write. Shortly after eating, mom and Otis (Odie) went for a walk. When they returned, Mom said to me, "Being as you can already read and write, we think that you could be more helpful by helping Odie with his work. You would learn a lot about automobiles and that might be more productive in later life than book learning." All of a sudden, I was wondering if I should have come back.

Soon I learned that I was back in the prayer meeting, revival world. We would attend church on Sunday mornings and evenings, and there were two prayer meetings during the week. Living with my father, we went to church every Sunday morning and tried to absorb enough to last the week.

Once or twice a year, a tent revival would set up in town. During this period, we could say goodbye to home cooked meals and clean clothes.

Mom would be so tied up with the Lord's work that she would do volunteer work and cleanup at the revival during the day. All of us would go to the revival at night. The tents had no fans or air conditioning and, when there was a revival during the summer, it was sheer torture. A lot of people would stand outside and listen. Occasionally, people would pass out during the services. One was always suspicious, as it was popular in those days for women to faint, if they were doing it to get attention. Fainting often happened in other places than tent revivals.

Something I never quite understood was that my mom would get baptized every session. If there were two services in a day, she would get baptized twice. I always believed that when one was baptized, that showed that they had accepted Jesus Christ as their Savior and that all sins were cast aside. My mom was the sweetest person you would ever meet. This made me wonder just what terrible sins she would be committing in the time between meetings. It seemed to me that she spent her other hours in praising the Lord and caring for her family. I never understood what was going on.

Twice yearly, our church had outside baptismal services in a nearby pond. Those participating would be totally submerged in the water and held down by the minister until they were splashing and struggling so much he could no longer hold them. It seems a wonder that no one ever drowned. At least none that I knew.

We always ate well, though nothing too fancy. Mom had a nice garden and she always raised a few chickens and rabbits. We had plenty of eggs and fried chicken. Horace and I were always upset when we had stewed rabbit. We had given them all names and had played with them. To eat rabbit seemed like you'd killed a friend.

A couple of months after my arrival, a sister, Lois, was born in our house. She was a normal, healthy baby and it was fun having her there with us. Horace became the designated baby sitter while I helped Odie in his duties of town handyman.

I was learning a little about automobiles, even though I was not strong enough to change a tire or make a real heavy pull on a wrench. However, I learned the tools and always had the right one ready for Odie. My carpentry skills were also quite limited, as I could not saw a straight line or drive a nail.

Mom mentioned several times that she and Odie would someday like to move to Los Angeles where her brothers, John and Jim Porterfield, had moved. It seemed there were a lot of opportunities there. Mom had also heard that there was a revival set up near the Los Angeles River that operated the year round. It was very tempting, but of course, they did not have the money to up and move. So, they dreamed about it.

Odie became somewhat abusive of me as time passed. He just didn't have the patience to work with one my age. I guess he expected more help than I was able to give him. By the time I was nine, he had beaten me several times. I talked to my mom and told her that I was going to go back to my dad. She said she thought that might be best. I asked her if I could take Horace with me, as I figured that if I left he would be next in line to take abuse. Mom said, "No, but I promise you that if he (Odie) ever abuses any of the kids, he will be gone." I was delighted to be going back to Lampasas, but I hated to leave my mom in a miserable situation.

A few days later, I stood at the edge of town, but this time I had a small suitcase and did not need a note pinned to my shirt. It was 1907. I was nine years old and had been this route before. Mom, Russell, and Jan came with me to say goodbye. Before they had turned around to leave me, a car came by. I stuck out a thumb and the driver stopped and said, "Get in." I was going to get my first ride in an automobile.

Though it was quite noisy, the car was much more comfortable than the wagon to ride in and it was pretty fast. The driver told me he was going to Lomita. I could not believe my good luck. Lomita is only 20 miles from Lampasas. We made the trip in only three hours, stopping twice to put water in the radiator.

Within minutes of arriving in Lomita, a wagon with two teamsters aboard stopped and offered me a ride. They were headed for San Antonio and would be passing through Lampasas. I would be home in about three hours. This sure beat my first trip that took three days. This time, the trip was about eight hours, including time delays.

These two gentlemen were among the nicest I have ever met. One was called Josh and the other, Henry. They stopped at the general store in Lomita and bought a big bag of jerky. We chewed on that until we reached my father's place. They were in the short haul delivery business, a business that was giving way to the automobile and trains. Three years earlier, it had been long haul deliveries, but now there was still a limited demand for short haul deliveries.

Josh and Henry asked what I was going to do in Lampasas. I told them that I was kind of being shifted back and forth from my mom to my dad. I said, "What I really want is a job so I can take care of myself." Josh replied, "Son, if you ever get to San Antonio, be sure to look us up. We know a lot of people and might be able to help." This made me happy, but I couldn't imagine ever getting to San Antonio.

We turned down the driveway to my dad's place so they could water the horses. Dad came out of the house and was quite surprised to see me. He knew I was just leaving Rising Star that morning. He was surprised when I told him of my good fortune in getting to ride in an automobile most of the way. I introduced him to Josh and Henry. My father seemed to like them at once. I took care of the horses and Miss Lillie fixed dinner. After eating a good meal of beef, corn on the cob, and beans, my dad invited them to bed down there for the night.

They said they would take a rain check and stop in again, but they thought that if they pushed on, they could make it to San Antonio late that night. This would allow them to drum up some business the following day.

After saying goodbye to Josh and Henry and watching their wagon disappear, we sat as a family and talked. Miss Lillie, Russell, and Les were quite interested in my trip, especially the part about riding in the car. None of them had ever ridden in one. Dad had ridden in a few, but had never owned one. Lester was now five years old and, barely remembering me, had a lot of questions. I was introduced to the two new members of my family, both sisters. Sallie, age 2, and Lillie, age 1.

Dad took me by surprise when he told me that he had sold the place and was moving over to Coryell County where my grandfather had a place and was in need of help. My grandfather, James W.

Gotcher, was 67 years old and had a large herd of sheep. He no longer had the energy to take care of the place and wanted dad to help. Grandfather was to furnish them with a larger house to help with the increase in our family size. That was definitely needed. The move was to take place in about two weeks.

Russell showed me his new reader. He had passed the third grade and was getting ready for the fourth. Les would be going into the second grade. The fourth grade reader looked kind of hard, but I felt I could figure it out if I had the book for a while.

Russell, Les, and I slept in the loft during the next two weeks. I spent a lot of time thinking and wondering if I had messed up. I had really looked forward to returning to school in Lampasas and having things stay the same as when I had left. The changes weighed heavily on my mind. I also thought of the possibilities that Josh and Henry had raised about San Antonio. I was going to need to build up a little courage and have a long talk with my dad.

In the next few days, I helped dad as best I could. He had traded his old wagon, two calves, two pigs, and twenty chickens for another team of horses and a much better wagon. We had to deliver these things. A butcher shop in Lampasas bought the rabbits. We didn't tell Russell or Lester where they had gone.

There were very few items to pack for the trip: Miss Lillie's rocking chair, all the bedding, dishes and utensils, clothing, dad's guns, and a few more miscellaneous items.

The day before we were leaving, I finally worked up the courage to tell my dad that I didn't want to go to Coryell County with them. I told him that Josh and Henry had said they could probably find me something in San Antonio and I really wanted to start working.

I was expecting him to say no, or at least express displeasure with my desires, but instead, he said, "Jack, you have been a man since you were four years old. Your mom and I haven't been the best parents in the world for you, but I want you to know how very much I love you. A man has to do what he has to do. If you want to try that and it doesn't work out, I want you to get your butt back to us as fast as you can." That ended the conversation and we wrapped our arms around each other and held on for a long moment.

That evening at the dinner table, he told the family that I had decided not to go with them. Miss Lillie and Russell broke into tears and I was feeling very guilty.

We all got up early in the morning and ate some biscuits and jelly that Miss Lillie had fixed the night before. I helped dad harness up the horses and hook them to the wagon. The last few items were put in the wagon and it was parting time. Except for the baby girls, there were no dry eyes as the wagon headed northeast. I headed south. I walked backwards towards Lampasas until the wagon disappeared.

CHAPTER 3

THE SAN ANTONIO YEARS

I had not been in Lampasas for more than a few minutes when a friend of my father asked what I was doing in town. I told him I was heading for a job in San Antonio. He said that he was driving there in a couple of hours if I cared to wait. I was most happy to wait and it took almost two hours to get to the northern outskirts of San Antonio. We had just passed the J&H Livery Stable. I told the driver that I needed off right here. He stopped. I thanked him and walked back half a block to the stable.

I found Henry at the stable. Josh was out on a local delivery. Henry was quite surprised and happy to see me. It was lunchtime and he fixed us each a sandwich.

After eating, Henry told me that they had talked about me after they let me off in Lampasas. They had decided that, if I ever showed up, they would hire me to look after things while they were making deliveries. They had an elderly man named Wilbert who had been handling this chore. However, he was often not available and, due to his age, they worried that he would get hurt.

Henry said, "We'll discuss it when Josh gets back, but you might as well put your clothes in the tack room in the stable. We'll set the harness and such in the barn and drive some nails in the wall to hang it on. I think there is an old army cot in there someplace and we'll get you some blankets. You can come in the house anytime you want. But, help yourself to anything in here."

Josh returned about 2:00 p.m., talked to Henry for a minute, and said to me, "Jack, we need some help here. Someone to watch the place when we are both out on deliveries. There are also horses and dogs around here that need food and water and the stable needs to be kept reasonably clean. We will also need you to put up the horses and soap the tack when we come in. Would you be willing to do that, and a few other chores, for room and board and two dollars a week?" I did not have to think at all. A shelter, food, and money, too. "Yes, Sir," I replied, and the bargain was struck.

Henry told me, "I'll let Wilbert know that we won't be needing him anymore and I am sure he will be happy about that. We both have two or three local runs to make tomorrow and will want to get out of her early, say around seven. So, if you feed and water the animals this evening and shake the gear out in the morning, we'll hitch up and be on our way."

We had a nice dinner of left over stew and bread and talked for a while. They were surprised that my dad had moved over to Coryell County, as he hadn't mentioned a move to them. They told me that business was pretty good, though it was almost always short hauls to cities not on the rail lines. Josh said that their business would be dying as more trucks became available. There were not enough trucks to go around yet, so things too big for cars, and without a rail line, would still use horses and wagons.

I was up at dawn doing my chores with vim and vigor. I knew how to hitch a team and Henry was surprised that, by the time they finished breakfast, everything was ready to go. I made a couple of minor repairs on one of the harnesses and greased the wheel hubs. I had made up my mind that I would do a good job for them. I also decided that I would send two dollars a month to my mom to help her out a bit.

It was 1908 and San Antonio was a hustling city of about 20,000 people. It had street cars, a ferry to cross the river, and a railroad that later became part of Southern Pacific railroad lines. It was about as modern as you could get at the time. (At least, this was true in the eyes of a ten year old.) It had the reputation of being a tourist city. There was always a lot going on there.

In 1909, the Pawnee Bill Wild West Show came to town and Josh and Henry took me to see this spectacular show. It featured cowboys doing tricks on their horses, a mock war between about 50 Indians in full dress and a like number of cowboys dressed in soldier uniforms. In many ways, this show and the Buffalo Bill Cody Wild West Show were the forerunners of the modern day rodeo.

A year later on my 12th birthday, Josh and Henry took me out to an airfield on the outskirts of San Antonio. I would witness one of the first air shows in Texas. I was quite impressed and returned home that evening not knowing if I wanted to be a pilot or a cowboy.

As I grew a bit and got more familiar with the surroundings, they began having me make some deliveries. I enjoyed getting away and seeing the sites. It helped them to have some time to relax, as age was not on their side. I had faithfully sent two dollars a month to my mom.

In 1911, I was 13 and could not believe what I got for Christmas. They took me out to the barn and there was a small cutting horse with a saddle and bridle. Also, a card under the tree read that my wages would now be five dollars a week. If I got a raise, my mom would get one and I promptly sent her five dollars.

In early January, 1912, Josh and Henry got an offer from someone wanting to buy the business and they accepted. It was obvious that trains and trucks were making a big impact on wagon deliveries. The sale would be finalized on the last day of the month. Work was a little slow and we spent some quality time together.

When the time came, we parted with much love and the usual promises to get back together soon. I think we realized that we probably would never see each other again. I prayed for their continued wellbeing. I had some decisions to make.

CHAPTER 4

KINGSVILLE AND COWBOY WAYS

In many ways, I was pleased that Josh and Henry had sold out. I know I never would have quit my job with them. I had a nest egg of about two hundred dollars after six years there, but I was still quite young and there was plenty of time.

I debated as to whether I should take a little time off, go visit my dad in Coryell County and my mom in Rising Star, or if I should try to find a job and hope that I could get some time off a little bit later in the year. I decided on the latter and rode into San Antonio. I heard rumors that they were hiring cowboys for the spring roundup at the King Ranch. Deciding to take a chance, I rode my horse to Kingsville. I took five days to make the 100-plus mile trip, enjoying the flowers along the way.

Kingsville was quite a place. It had only about 300 residents, but it had a sewage system, lights and power, and running water. It had just been named as the county seat for the newly formed Kleberg County. There was a notice at the Post Office saying, "Wanted: All types of ranch hands for work at King Ranch. Drifters not wanted. See Ed Duggan for details." I found Mr. Duggan near the rail yard and talked with him. He said, "Aren't you a little young, Jack?" I lied to him and said that I was almost sixteen (I would be fourteen in June), and that I could ride, rope, and take care of equipment.

He paused for a moment and said, "Well, I'd rather teach someone who was willing than to hire some of these guys who know it all, but won't do any of it. Let's ride over to the office and I'll sign you on. I can start you right away for thirty dollars a month. If you make good and I keep you after roundup, we will raise it to forty or so. However, I must warn you. We keep very few gringos, as our Mexican's are good cowboys and get along well here. Your biggest job will be loading rail cars with cattle driven in from the northern range. That looks like a pretty good little cutting horse you have there, but when we get busy, you will need to change horses several times a day. So, you had best put your horse in the small back pasture and leave him there for your personal pleasure. We have the best horses, cattle, and sheep in the world, and we don't really like them mixing. If you don't have any questions, go over to the hotel and tell them I sent you. They will put you into a shared room until we figure exactly how you'll be used."

The King Ranch was, and still is, the biggest ranch in the U. S., and has ranged from a low of around 900,000 acres to well over a million acres. It is larger than the state of Rhode Island. A rough estimate was that it had forty to fifty thousand head of cattle, over six thousand horses, and fifteen thousand sheep. Farm wagons were being replaced with trucks, but I would guess we had three or four dozen of each. Massive is all I can say about the place.

The ranch was split into three sections, the south area was called the Norias and had the majority of the cattle. The other two areas had a mixture of everything.

Richard King, a steamboat captain, had started developing the ranch 100 years earlier. Apparently, he had no sons, but one of his daughters married an energetic attorney named Bob Kleberg. So, the Kleberg name became the ruling family. Despite their tremendous wealth, they were very hard working people and very knowledgeable about the ranch. They wanted to own, and did own, the finest line of horses and cattle to be found anywhere.

A story went around the ranch that, at one time, the outlaw, Jesse James, had visited the ranch using an assumed name. He was treated well by the Klebergs and he appreciated the hospitality. The Klebergs admired his horse. The story goes that, once he got off the King property, he traded horses with his escort and told him to take it back and tell them that the horse was a gift from Jesse James.

At least 90% of the workforce was made up of Mexicans. They mostly worked with the cattle and there were some fine cowboys among them. They were as good as they came. When they were herding cattle, they worked as a team with very little communications. They just knew where they belonged or what they should be doing.

I worked with the group assigned to load the cattle onto rail cars at the main ranch. The main roundup had already started and we were busy from the get go. This job was fairly easy. We would drive the cattle into a corral and then on to a wide opening that narrowed down to where the only exit was to the ramp leading into the rail car. There was hay throughout the rail car and the cattle would start eating immediately. This would keep them calm. Occasionally, we would be looking for breeding stock for a special order. Ed usually picked them out and I would cut them out and into a holding corral for later shipment to a customer. Those picked would not be shipped to Kansas City for slaughter. Although all stock on the King Ranch was fine, the selected ones were the finest of the fine. When I wasn't helping with this, I was told to jump in and help wherever I could.

I was getting pretty good with a lariat. I learned that there is a bit of glory in work. If you are cutting out the cow or bull for a special reason, you must do so without disturbing the rest of the herd. When you are doing your job well, the other workers take notice and begin to cheer quite mildly. You always hope the boss or one of the Kleberg's would be around when you were working well. That would bring on recognition.

I will never forget the slow, even pace of the roundup. Oxen were used on the flank when the herd was pretty well gathered and being driven in. These big beasts are slow, calm movers and have a definite calming effect on the herd. I never saw this done anyplace but the King Ranch, but then, no one else ever handled herds the size that they did there.

My roping and riding were getting better and better all the time. The ranch kept me on after the layoff in April and promptly raised my salary to forty dollars a month. I always sent my mom ten dollars, and sometimes twenty. She was most appreciative, but I hoped that she was buying things for the family and not putting it all into the church offering collection dish.

One evening, Ed Duggan, my foreman, approached me and called me aside. He said, "Jack, you've been with us a little over a year now. You can handle a rope better than anyone else on the ranch. In fact, you handle it better than anyone I've seen in those Wild West travelling shows. I sometimes compare you with Will Rogers. I saw him once and, except for the fact that he was a good comedian, he had nothing on you. Your riding is pretty good, too. I was wondering if you had ever been to a rodeo or knew enough about it to want to ride in one." I had never been to a rodeo, as they were just coming of age. I certainly had heard of frontier days in Cheyenne, Wyoming. This event had been going on for about ten years and was getting bigger every year. I had heard from some drifters that they were going to start a big one in Calgary, Alberta, in the near future. Also, the Fort Worth Cattleman's Association was making some moves to have their own rodeo. But my answer to Ed was that I sure would like to ride in one.

Ed said, "Jack, this weekend, there is a rodeo in Laredo. If you would like to ride over with me Saturday, we can get entered and you would ride on Sunday. You pick your events and I will pay the entry fee. If you win, we will split. I asked, "What time do we leave?" His reply was, "Around 10:00 a.m."

Saturday morning, we got onto his motorcycle with a sidecar and took off. I had never ridden on a motorcycle before. I could not believe that we made the 126-mile trip in 3 hours. Ed knew right where to go and we checked into a hotel above a bar. I thought we would share a room, but Ed said we needed separate rooms. I went to my room, looked around for a tub, and found it. It was a galvanized tub. However, no water was connected to it meaning someone would have to bring me hot water. I had not been in the room very long when a pretty senorita knocked on the door. She said, "I'll be with you tonight."

On occasion, Henry and Josh had taken me to a cathouse in San Antonio, but that was only for a quickie. I had never spent the night with a woman, especially a very pretty one. We had just had our first session when Ed knocked on the door and said, "Come on, Jack. We need to get you signed up." I slipped on my jeans and a shirt and was on the way downstairs.

There were a couple of large men wearing nice Stetson hats sitting at a table with Ed. It was obvious that they were signing up contestants for the following day's events. Ed thought I was a cinch in the calf roping and saddle bronc riding events and signed me up for those. The entry fee was ten dollars for each event, but the prizes were fifty dollars each. If I only won one event, we would barely break even for the trip, hotel rooms, and entry fee. I began to feel a little bit of pressure. In either event, a lazy horse or a stumbling calf would mean failure.

Unknown to me, Ed had also entered me in two other events: bareback bronco busting and bull riding. He must have known something. It seemed to me that forty dollars on an unknown was risky. Even for a ranch foreman, that was a lot of money, or so I thought.

Ed and I sat there for a while and had a couple of drinks. He was constantly wandering over to the other tables to greet others. When not doing this, others were coming over to us. Ed seemed to know everyone. I think he either read boredom or lust in my eyes.

He finally said, "Jack, why dong you go on upstairs and get some rest for tomorrow?" I didn't have to be asked twice.

I returned to my room for an adventurous night with my Mexican beauty. She had room service fill the tub with water while I was gone and directed me to get into it. I didn't really need to; I had bathed at Kingsville a couple of days before.

We woke up Sunday morning to a warm spring day. The parade through downtown Laredo to the fairgrounds would start at 11:00 a.m. It consisted of the school band, a couple of riding teams, a group of Texas Rangers, and the rodeo queen. She obviously had political influence and a charming personality, as looks did not seem to have been a priority. Some other groups rode at the back of the parade, but they were disorganized and it was impossible to recognize them.

The bull riding event was the first of the rodeo. I was not scheduled to be in this event, but I was becoming aware that Ed had entered me in a couple of extra events. I guess he was trying to insure getting some of the entry money back. A 15-year old doesn't really tell his boss, "No way!" This is especially true if he figures that he has the best job in the world and wants to keep it.

I was fortunate enough to come in second. That paid fifteen dollars, so I felt good that I had gotten some of Ed's money back. I also realized that I had better hang around the corral and be available for other events. We had agreed that I would enter the bronco riding and calf roping contests.

The bronco riding event was the next thing I was called for. I got a very good horse who gave a very good ride. If you were a good rider, the horse would determine the winner. Luck would be on my side; I would win that one. A win of first place paid fifty dollars and I was happy to report to the stands and get that cash.

I came in second in the bareback bronc riding. I think there were only four entrants. Two of them were younger than me. I learned later that I was a last minute entry. When Ed found out there wasn't a lot of competition, I was in it. This gave us eighty dollars in winnings with my best event, calf roping, still coming up.

By the time I caught my wind, they announced that the calf roping would be the next contest. This was what I thought would be my best event and it turned out that way. I had roped and tied my calf almost out of the chute. As I was the first one to participate in that event, I had to watch while seven other riders went for it. A couple of them did pretty good and I was a little worried at the end, as timing was not an art at this stage of the rodeo world. Loud speakers were unknown at the time and the man who did the announcing used a large megaphone. He announced, "Jack Gotcher has just set a new world's record in calf roping with a time of 7.9 seconds. Come on up here, Jack." I loved the roar of the crowd and it was loud since they had said it was a new world's record.

I believe they used a windup alarm clock to time these events. I was to learn later in life that it was customary to set a world's record at all rodeos. Not a lot of record books were kept and records would go up and down. If they got too low, then they would have taken no time at all. Regardless, I was happy to go up and pick up the fifty dollars. It would give me something to write home about.

I was getting ready to take the horse back to the stable and grab my saddle when another announcement was made. "Will Jack Gotcher please report to the judge's stand?" "Oh, oh", I thought to myself. "They must be disqualifying me from something. What could I have done wrong?" As I arrived at the booth not knowing what to expect, the announcer said, "Ladies and Gentlemen, here he is, our Best All-Around Cowboy, Jack Gotcher! Here, Jack, is your hundred dollars. Let's hear it for Jack. We also have a plaque to be engraved with his name that we'll send to Kingsville when the engraving is done." I didn't know whether to faint or cry; this was totally unexpected.

I had been mentally figuring that the split with Ed would give me sixty-five dollars, but now there was another fifty to add to it. Now, it appeared that I would have one hundred thirty-five dollars.

Not bad for a boy in his first rodeo who only made forty dollars a month for working twelve hours a day, six to seven days a week.

When I got back to the hotel, Ed was sitting in the bar bragging about me, saying, "Jack's the kind of cowboy we have at the King Ranch." I was really proud. I handed him the winnings and he counted and then handed one hundred sixty-five dollars back to me. I told him that he had shorted himself, that he had fifty more dollars coming. He would have none of that. His words were, "I entered you in all the events except for that one. You went out and won that by yourself." I didn't feel right in accepting it until he assured me that he had won over four hundred dollars betting on me against people from other ranches.

We entered several other small rodeos that year and usually walked away with around one hundred dollars or more. It was a lot of fun and I was able to send quite a bit of money home to my mom.

There had always been a lot of bandits in southern Texas during this time. It seemed to be on the increase in 1914. Some of these were Mexican bandits sent to replenish money for their leader, one Pancho Villa. Others were just plain thieves from the U.S. Those of us working in and around Kingsville were relatively safe. The big house was fortified and could have held off an army.

We saw more and more Texas Rangers come onto the scene and these guys always seemed to get their man. It was rumored that most of the men they caught were killed trying to escape, but that might just be a story. I believe it was 1915 when the last noteworthy raid was made on King land.

During these years, life remained simple and much the same. I did get a raise to fifty dollars a month, which made me feel like a top hand. I had learned a lot about calle, horses, sheep, and ranching. Ed had been a great influence on me. He was like another dad to me. We continued to do the rodeo circuit after the first roundup and worked our butts off, otherwise.

Entertainment was scarce and we spent some spare time pitching horse shoes. Occasionally, we would pass the King Mansion and they would be playing Croquet on the lawn. None of the cowboys knew anything about that game.

In the middle of 1916, there was a big rodeo in San Antonio. I believe that Ed and others approached the Klebergs about having some of the cowboys from Kings Ranch enter. They were all for the idea and paid our entry fees. They also furnished a bus for us to go to San Antonio. I told Ed that I would still split my winnings with him. He said, "Forget it. Just ride your best and we'll make plenty on bets." I placed first in calf roping, an event that paid one hundred dollars. I placed second in both the saddle bronc busting and the bull riding events. They each paid fifty dollars, so I now had two hundred dollars in winnings. Members of the Kleberg family matched our winnings, so that gave me four hundred dollars. I knew they were going to give an award for the outstanding cowboy and part of me felt that I had a good chance. Sure enough, I got called and was prepared to collect a few more dollars. I certainly was not disappointed when the prize turned out to be a new saddle. I thought I would keep it forever.

During the two days I was in San Antonio, I wandered around the town a bit, even to the area where Josh and Henry had the stable. I asked a neighboring business if they knew anything about what had become of them. They did not know for sure, but thought they might have gone to Alabama and retired. The business had been closed for some time. It was kind of sad, but a sign of progress.

During my travels, I had seen a store where they had a used Indian motorcycle for sale. It had a sidecar and was a lot like Ed's. They were asking two hundred ninety-five dollars for it. I tried it out and it seemed to be okay. At the time I looked at it, I did not have or know what my winnings would be, but now armed with four hundred dollars, I made a B-line back there. I negotiated a bit and got them to go down to two hundred fifty dollars. I rode off on it.

The Klebergs suggested that we spend another night in San Antonio and not return to the ranch until Monday. We were unanimous in agreement with our generous employer. I hadn't looked forward to a night ride my first time out on the motorcycle. I left very early on Monday morning to be sure I was ahead of the bus, in case the bike had a problem. I think I hit every pothole in the road and it was pretty bumpy. I was sure glad I didn't have to make that first trip at night time. Fortunately, the motorcycle ran quite well and I felt that I had made a good investment.

There was a bad drought in 1916. We lost a lot of cattle, horses, and sheep. In our daily duties, we ate a lot of dust....a lot of dust. It began to cool down a bit in the fall and we had branding, dehorning, and castrating the animals among our chores. It had been a rough spring and summer, a new record for the most days without rain. One really learned why cowboys wear kerchiefs. We seldom had them off our nose and mouth. Still, the dust was so thick that it was difficult to see more than ten feet in any direction. The sun was seldom seen.

Rain finally came and the fall roundup went quite well. However, due to the drought and lack of food, many of the cattle would have to be held back until the following roundup. They were just plain too thin.

Entertainment was a bit hard to come by. Telephone, TV, or movies were not available.

There was a rumor that, in the big house, the Kings had a radio which would pick up New York and England, but no one I knew had ever seen it. So, once it was dark, music became our source of entertainment. There was usually someone who could play a fiddle. We had a guitar player and a couple of us played harmonica, but I was usually told to yodel or whistle. I wasn't too bad at either. One of our favorite songs was "Tweedle Twill". Songs like "The Blue Tail Fly," "Jimmy Cracked Corn", and "Little Joe the Wrangler" were also among our favorites. We sang them whenever enough of us could get together. Due to the fact our work was scattered out, that wasn't too often.

In 1917, The United States declared war on Germany and we were sending troops off to Europe. Right after the January roundup was finished, my cousin, Burl Porterfield, came to Kingsville for a visit. His parents, the Jim Porterfields, and our Uncle John's family had moved to Ontario, California. He said that my mother wanted to move out there, too. He brought five letters to me.

The first letter I opened was from my mom, thanking me for all the help I had been. She told me that she and Odie had gotten divorced and she was now remarried. They were going to have a baby later in the year. Of seemingly more importance was a note that said my name had been placed on the message board at the Rising Star Post Office. It said that I needed to come in and register for Selective Service.

The other three letters were of a different nature. I was quite surprised by their content. The Fort Worth Cattlemen's Association, the Guthrie, Oklahoma Rodeo and Livestock Show, and the Cheyenne, Wyoming Frontier Days all invited me to participate in their rodeos that spring. Each rodeo would allow me to enter any event I cared to enter without an entry fee. I would have some decisions to make, but not that day.

One of the cowboys from the Norias range recognized my cousin, Burl. Later that day, Ed saw me and asked how long Burl would be staying. I thought maybe they wanted him to leave and I said, "He can leave tonight if they would like." He then told me the Klebergs wanted Burl, Ed, and me to dine with them the following evening. It would be the next night before I would find out what that was all about.

After a day of work a bath, and putting on my best clothes, Burl, Ed, and I headed for the Mansion, not knowing what was happening, but feeling that it would be something good. We arrived and were taken to a sitting room where we wer introduced to various male and female members of the ruling family. I seemed to get a lot of attention at first, as the San Antonio rodeo was still on some of their minds. Then, the attention turned to Burl.

Burl was a very talented musician, in addition to other things. He was great on the piano and violin, and could also play a good tune on the saw. Someone who had heard him play had recognized him. They told the Klebergs and this was a command performance. Burl was shown a "Baby Grand Piano", so elegant that he was almost afraid to touch it. These pianos were the gems of that, or any other, era. He played a little classical and some popular western ballads. Everyone was dumbfounded at his talents. This clean, but poorly dressed gypsy, had brought some life to that sitting room.

We were called to the formal dining room. It, like the rest of the house, was more elegant than any I had ever seen, or probably ever would see. The dinner was great, though there were many dishes that both Burl and I felt uneasy with, as we didn't know what we were eating. However, we made it through the evening without any mishaps.

After dinner, it was back to Burl and the piano. After four or five numbers, he got out a violin and began to fiddle. Man, he was good! Ed and one of the Klebergs were talking, and Ed then left the house. He returned a short time later with a saw, so we would see Burl play this instrument. It took some talent, but it was great amusement in the era. It seemed an impossible task to most of those who had tried it. It consisted of using a regular wood saw and, by bending the blades, it would send out different notes. A master like Burl could change the notes, develop rhythm, and play a pretty fair tune. There were about 20 people in the sitting room enjoying the performance, laughing, and being amazed by it all. After the saw, he played a couple of tunes on his harmonica and then asked for a guitar. I began to realize that Burl was a master showman. He played one song on the guitar, then told the audience, "My cousin, Jack, is one of the best at yodeling you will ever hear." I was embarrassed, but knew of no way out. He played a couple of songs, I yodeled, then he returned to the piano for one last medley. We thanked our gracious host and they thanked us. They told us to come back anytime. I my mind, I thought, "Oh, yeah, anytime. I'll probably come for breakfast, ha, ha!"

However, Burl was called to the big house the following day. They offered him a job to play for a couple of hours each afternoon and evening. There would not necessarily be people where he was playing. He was to just play and, if someone wanted to listen and relax, so be it. They offered him twenty-five dollars a week. He told them that he wouldn't be there too long. They said that was alright and he accepted. They sent him to their tailor shop to have a little better outfit made. Within a day or so, you would not recognize him, my well-dressed cousin from Rising Star.

I was facing the crisis. It was obvious that I needed to go to Rising Star and register for the draft. The rodeo invitations were tempting, but I would never be able to take time off work for them. If I didn't take off, was I missing a chance to be a world class cowboy? I thought and thought and still didn't find an answer. I needed to have a heart to heart talk with Ed Duggan. He would know what was best.

I told Ed of the need to go home to register and of the rodeo opportunities. Ed said to me, "Let's go inside and sit down. We need to have a real long talk." And a long talk it was.

Ed said, "Jack, you are a top young hand, one of the best we have ever had at Kingsville. I can give you a week off, but an indefinite leave is out of the question. Mr. Flowers, over in the Norias range, has spoken about moving you over there. He has way too much ground to cover and, even though his Vaqueros foreman is great, they have a need for more management to cover that area. Then, in four or five years, I will be stepping down and someone will be taking my place. We have talked about you as a replacement. We all agreed that you would be ready for it. That would be a big promotion, and a lot of responsibility goes with it. As far as you making it big on the rodeo circuit, you are real good. But, the competition around here is in no way what you will run into at Fort Worth and Guthrie. Most of those guys are rodeo bums. They just barely survive, but they are good at what they do. To be honest with you, I think you would be extremely lucky to place in any event at either place. I think you should have fun with your riding and roping abilities at these area events and look at the big picture for your future. Your opportunities here at Kingsville far outnumber what they might be on the rodeo circuit. I will keep quiet now, but I really hope you will make a wise decision."

I didn't! After tossing and turning all night, I made my decision to go. I went to Ed and gave him two weeks' notice. He thanked me for the good things I had done at the ranch and for our friendship. He said, "Jack, if you ever need a job, contact me. The Klebergs don't really like rehiring people who are progressing and then up and quit, but just maybe they would make an exception in your case."

I began realizing the finality of what I was doing, but it was time to get going. When the two weeks passed, I sold my horse and made arrangements to ship my saddle and a few personal things to Rising Star.

My cousin, Burl, would leave with me, as he was a bit homesick already. I think they were going to miss him more than me. He had brought a definite sparkle to the big house. We said our goodbyes and headed north.

On the long trip north, I thought about some of the humorous things I had learned at King Ranch. Burl and I laughed about them. A few of our memories included:

1. Never squat with your spurs on.
2. When riding in front of the herd, look back and make sure it is still there.
3. Always drink upstream of the herd.
4. Never miss a chance to shut up.
5. There are a lot of ideas on handling women. None of them work.
6. If you find yourself in a hole, quit digging.
7. Don't kick a cow chip when it's hot.
8. Good judgment comes from experience and a lot of that experience comes from bad judgment.
9. The only difference between a rut and a grave is the depth.

10. If God wanted me to touch my toes, he would have put them on my knees.

Knowledge of things like these would be helpful throughout my life.

CHAPTER 5

HOME AND BEYOND

The family was certainly trying to be self-supporting. Skinny and Fletch were both working when something was available, but four to five dollars a month was about all they could make. Jan and Lois occasionally got babysitting jobs, but that only paid 25 cents for an evening, or a dollar for an entire weekend. My stepfather, carrying on the tradition of Mom's last three husbands, was a town handyman who didn't seem to care to do a lot. He lacked in mechanical skills, so available jobs were limited.

I gave my mom two hundred fifty dollars, the most money she had ever seen. She was afraid that I was a wanted man. Mom went right out and bought nine dollars' worth of groceries. This was a huge amount for someone who had their own garden, plus rabbits and poultry in their yard. We would eat well for a couple of days.

I learned that my father had packed up again and moved the family from Coryell County over to the Odessa-Midlands area. I wanted to get over to see them, but decided to wait until after the Fort Worth rodeo. It was still a couple of weeks away.

I thought that I had better get down to the draft board. Mom told me that there was a lady at the Post Office who handled the registrations. I drove my motorcycle the three blocks to the Post Office and cruised up and down the street several times, hoping everyone would look at me and realize that Jack must be doing quite well. It was important to me for them to think I was a success. After all, out branch of the Porterfields were known to be quite poor.

In the Post Office, I was handed a blurred printed form to fill out. It was the Selective Service form of the era. It was not a complicated form. It asked for name, age, address, and had a couple of questions as to any reason you might not be able to serve in the military.

Even with my limited reading skills, I went through it pretty well. However, I did make one mistake. The form questioned age. I thought they meant the year born and entered the numbers 98.

The days passed quickly and, before I knew it, the time arrived to head to Fort Worth. It would be strange entering an event without Ed Duggan there to coach me. There was a barn set up in the stockyards for the cowboys to stay in. I found a couple of bales of hay in a corner and set up to stay a few days.

On the day before the rodeo, a lot of the guys were drunk and just hanging around. There was a small stakes card game that I entered and won almost five dollars. Heck, I could have gotten a hotel room and eaten with this kind of money. I knew I was ready for the big time rodeo. I signed up for bareback riding, saddle bronco busting, calf roping, and bull riding.

The morning of the rodeo arrived. Temperatures were mild and it would be ideal weather to ride. The parade from downtown to the stockyards was fairly long and, due to delays, the rodeo did not start until 2:30 p.m. It had been scheduled to begin at 1:00 p.m.

It was customary for the cowboys to furnish their own personal clothing, chaps, and lariat. Other than that, everything was furnished by the association. This made events like calf roping or steer wrestling a bit more difficult to those accustomed to using their own horse and saddle. The luck of what horse you drew could overcome your personal skills. Of course, in other events, a lazy bull or an overactive horse could put you out, too.

The grandstand was packed with howling fans, all having their favorites. They would jeer or boo, as well as cheer and applaud. The first three events I entered did not go well for me, though I still had some enthusiasm. The final event would be my specialty: calf roping.

My horse was calm in the chute, even after I lowered myself onto the saddle. I was hoping that he would show a little more fire, but it would not have mattered. The calf was released. It did not break far out of the chute when it made a sharp left at the same time we came out of the chute. My horse tripped and that was it for the day. Thank goodness, neither the horse nor the calf were hurt.

They then announced that the winner of the calf roping event had just set a new world's record of 8.2 seconds. This was .3 of a second slower than my old world record that had been set in my very first rodeo. Timing was not yet a sophisticated tool.

That evening, I stayed in the stable and gave a lot of thought to what Ed had told me. I got to feeling he was more right than wrong, but I would need to try a couple of more rodeos with the pros.

Late that evening, someone came by and offered me a job to help clean up the grounds for a couple of days. It would pay three dollars a day. I accepted the job and worked for two days. That six dollars, along with my poker winnings, put me a couple of dollars ahead.

I returned to Rising Star for a night. I told my mom that I was going on to Odessa to see my dad. I wanted to start early, as it was about 240 miles of hot, summer driving.

Leaving Rising Star about 5:30 a.m., I arrived in Odessa just before noon. I grabbed a quick lunch while inquiring about where I would find my dad. Odessa was just beginning to be an oil town, but most of the ranches around were raising sheep. It was on such a ranch, north of town, where I found my father. He had about 200 acres, a herd of sheep, and goats. My stepmom, Miss Lillie, was raising the usual: rabbits, chickens, and a garden.

The family had grown a lot since I last saw them. There had been two more brothers, Murray, age 6, and Todd, age 3. Russell was 18 and Les, 16. The girls, Fannie and Lilly, were now teenagers and both were really good looking girls. I would have been proud to take either one of them out if they had not been my sisters.

I arrived on a Saturday afternoon and received lots of hugs. It had been a long time since I had seen them. The girls would not remember me and, of course, Murray and Todd had never seen me. I was told that the whole family would be going to the dance that evening. Dad had bought a Ford Model T and there would not be room for everyone in it. Russell and I rode to the dance on my motorcycle.

No one had said anything, so I was quite surprised when my brother, Les, was the caller at the square dance. He was really good and was paid two dollars, plus tips for his efforts. Russell and I just stood around with the single guys, eyeballing a couple of gals, but couldn't really make eye contact. We tried standing by the punch bowl for quite a while, but they didn't bother to come over.

I stayed around for three or four days doing some bonding with my father and the rest of the family. The trip to Guthrie, Oklahoma, would be about 400 miles. So, about five days before the Guthrie rodeo, I said my goodbyes and hit the road. I arrived in Oklahoma City late on my second day of travel. I got a cabin in Oklahoma City, which is about 40 miles south of Guthrie.

On the Friday before the rodeo, I drove my motorcycle up to Guthrie to look things over. One of the first things I noticed was that a lot of cowboys had come in on rail cars with their own horses. The Rodeo Association rules clearly stated that all horses and other livestock would be furnished by the Association. I learned that this rule was pretty much waivered in the calf and steer roping contests. I thought how nice it would be if I still had my horse, but that would have been difficult with my motorcycle. I guess we could have made it by rail. It is more than a little rough, going into a timed contest with a strange animal as your partner.

The Guthrie rodeo had a larger crowd than the one in Fort Worth. People came from all over Texas, Arkansas, Kansas, and Oklahoma for this event. Competition seemed a little fiercer than in other places. I was able to finish third place in two events, for a total of thirty dollars. I felt reasonably good on my showing, though was once again disappointed when I did not place in the calf roping event. Once again, a new world's record was set in this event. It was the same time, 8.2 seconds, as had been recorded in Fort Worth two weeks prior, but now I understood.

There would be a rodeo in Wichita the following weekend and, as Wichita was only 130 miles north, I decided to go up that way and enter.

I didn't really expect to win at Wichita, but surprised myself with a second place in calf roping and a third in steer roping. That meant a fifty dollar payday.

The next event would be in Cheyenne Wyoming, then Calgary, Alberta. After a lot of thinking, I thought it best that I get back to ranch and some of the smaller rodeos. I was seeing a lot of older guys, too old to compete, but still trying. This was all they knew and they had nothing else. I was 19 now and there were some 16- and 17-year olds who were very good at competing.

I gave some thought to sending a wire to Ed Duggan in Kingsville, but just could not do it. Pride, or whatever, was stopping me. So, it was time to go to work. I did enter a rodeo in Colorado Springs a couple of weeks later and won three of the four events that I entered. This paid me seventy-five dollars, enough spending money for a month.

I went over around Lamar, Colorado, and took a job on a dirt farm. It paid me three dollars a day, plus room and board. I was doing a lot of plowing. The ranch only had two plow horses, so there was no way for me to polish my riding skills. To stay sharp with the lariat, I would run as fast as I could while twirling the rope and lassoing fence posts or sage brush. It was a lot different from the real thing, but it was good exercise and helped me retain the feel

CHAPTER 6

BESSIE

In early September, I went into Lamar to register for their fall rodeo which was to be held on October 17th. They told me that the man at the feed and grain store was accepting entry fees. I was quite surprised when he said, "I don't recall your last name, but they call you Jack. Am I right?" I nodded, and he said, "I saw you ride in Wichita a couple of months ago. You are just the shot in the arm we need here. Would you mind if we publicize your entry?" I didn't really understand what he meant, but I gave him my okay. He then took me over to the local photography shop and had a picture taken of me.

Two weeks later on another visit to town, I saw a poster which had my picture on it. The poster read, "Lamar Rodeo, Sunday, October 17, 1:30 p.m. Special guest: Jack Gotcher of the Professional Rodeo Association. Jack will also demonstrate his unique skills of roping."

I didn't know if I was excited or scared the most. Here I was, expected to draw in spectators as well as perform. I was not Will Rogers, but I would do my best.

Shortly after the pre-rodeo events started, I got one big extra thrill. A group of young people, with pens in hand, requested my autograph. This was truly the big time. I did a good job; my handwriting was so poor that it looked like a real professional signature.

When the barrel race was completed, the announcer called on Jack Gotcher of Rising Star, Texas, to give a roping exhibition. I started off chasing and roping a few wild calves that were turned loose for me. Then, a rider would race around the corral with me chasing him. I would lasso him and pull him to the ground. This went over well. I closed out the event with a bit of rope twirling while riding, first creating a large loop over my head. Eventually, I lowered myself off the horse with the rope still twirling over my head. I then lowered the twirling loop to where it was around my body a few inches above my ankles. The crowd loved this and threw coins out in the corral. I got over seventeen dollars from their generosity.

The rodeo was ready to begin and the side shows stopped. I won three of the four events I entered. The calf and steer roping contests were won without much sweat. I also did well in the bull riding, getting a first place. I did not place in the saddle bronc riding.

For the first time ever, I entered and rode as an out rider in the chuck wagon race. It was fun, but my bunch didn't place. In this event, several wagons raced around the track with a company of four riders. It is a fast and furious paced event. Riders get mixed with others. The first wagon to complete the race with all their riders finishing wins the event. A wagon can come in third, but if its riders are along with it, then it is the winner. It is noted that the riders must stay behind their chuck wagon and never pass it. This is always one of the favorite events of the crowd.

Looking into the crowd, I saw a beautiful, dark haired gal and tried unsuccessfully to catch her eye. I just had to find a way to meet her. The last event of the day was the bareback bronc riding. I went over to the judge's booth and asked if I could still enter. They were only too happy to accommodate me. They only had three entries and that meant, that unless a fourth was found, everyone was a winner.

The previous day, we had a chance to work out with the animals being used. I had noticed this one bronco who continually turned right and began bucking right out of the chute. I asked if I could have that one and was told that I could because the draw had already been completed for the three previous entrants.

When my turn to ride came up, I was hoping so much that this horse would do as he had done on the previous day. I was not disappointed. We came out of the chute and he immediately turned a sharp right, almost dragging me on the edge of the fence. He began bucking furiously and, at the right moment, I let go of the strap and went flying over the fence at the feet of the pretty lady. Getting up and shaking myself off, I asked if she was all right. She replied, "Yes, you didn't touch me." I apologized for the close call and introduced myself. "I'm Jack; what do they call you?" She said, "I'm Bessie. Bessie James." I asked if she would have a soda with me later after I picked up my winnings. She replied, "I live in La Junta and the stage doesn't leave until five, so I have about one and a half hours to kill. I guess it will be all right. I certainly am thirsty and a soda or iced tea would be nice."

My winnings were better than expected. I got twenty-five dollars for each of my first place finishes. They named me "Outstanding Cowboy" and gave me a saddle and a lariat. I had no use for either and promptly sold them for thirty-five dollars. The Rodeo Association gave me seventeen dollars for using my name and picture for advertising. That let me walk away with one hundred twenty-seven dollars.

I was a happy, young cowboy when I left the rodeo grounds and found young Bessie waiting for me at the gate. We had our sodas and then went for a walk. I learned quite a bit about her in our walk. She was twenty years old and lived with her parents. She worked almost full time as a substitute school teacher. Her parents were very strict with her and had threatened to disown her on several occasions.

In mentioning my dreams, I told her that I was a wandering cowboy and that some of my dreams were about my being a cattle baron. She said that she thought she would like to do some cattle ranching. We ducked back into the pharmacy where we had drunk our sodas when a brief rainstorm hit. It would have been nice if it had hit before the rodeo and helped to hold the dust down. We walked to the park and set on a bench watching a beautiful rainbow appear. I had been raised to believe there was a pot of gold at the end of a rainbow, but I was too busy talking to Bessie to chase this one down. I felt that, at the moment, she was the rainbow.

Suddenly, we both realized it was 5:30 p.m. We rushed to the bus stop, but the bus was long gone. I told her not to worry, we could jump on my motorcycle and be there almost as quick as the bus. She began to cry, telling me her mother would disown her for riding on a motorcycle. Nice girls just didn't do things like that. We walked some more and settled on a park bench. Suddenly, I said, "Bessie, will you marry me?" Without any hesitation, she replied, "Yes, Jack, I'd love to!" We attempted to get a room at the hotel, but were refused when we could not prove we were married. It was then back to the park for a night of sleeping on a bench. Luck was with us as that part of Colorado can get pretty cool in late October. It was a very nice night.

At 9:00 a.m., we were in the Justice of the Peace's office, got a marriage license, and were married all in motion. The total cost for the license and the marriage ceremony was five dollars. That included a one dollar tip for both the Justice of the Peace and his receptionist, who also served as our witness.

Now it was time to get on the motorcycle, ride to La Junta, and meet my new in-laws. I had no idea just what to expect, but it was obvious that Bessie dreaded the thought of it. She had every reason.

Her parents had a few acres about four miles out of La Junta. The roar of my motorcycle brought everyone to the front yard. Her mother flew into a rage, calling Bessie a tramp and a whore. She also told her to leave and never come back. She didn't even listen when Bessie tried to introduce me as her husband.

It seemed like her father wasn't in favor of this, but he stood silently by. Bessie went into the house and packed a suitcase. Her older brother, Harrison, tried to calm her mother down, but he had no luck. Bessie's mother was beyond control. Tom, her younger brother, just stood there somewhat bewildered.

It didn't look like Colorado was in our future, at least for a while, so we returned to Lamar. I got the few clothes I had packed. We took the saddle that I had won in San Antonio and a tack shop gave me forty-five dollars for it. I hated to give it up, but two people on a motorcycle with a side car don't have much room for all their worldly goods, plus a saddle.

I told Bessie that Wyoming and Montana had a lot of big cattle ranches and I thought we should head up there. By now, she was ready for anything that would get her away from her mother. It was obvious that she was deeply hurt.

On our trip north, we occasionally rented a cabin, as motels of that era were called. They usually had cooking facilities and Bessie showed that she was a pretty good cook, but was having difficulty buying just enough for one or two meals. We generally tried to drive until dark and, on a couple of occasions, we slept in the open near the road.

We checked out ranches in the Billings, Montana, and Cody, Wyoming, areas without any luck. The roundups were over and the cattle had all been driven to winter range. November is not a good time to look for outside work in either Wyoming or Montana. We heard tell of minus 50 degrees temperatures and felt that we had best head south…..way south!

The trip went pretty well. We hit some snow on a mountain pass between Billings and Cheyenne, but got through okay. After that, it was pretty easy and we made three overnight stops heading for Rising Star.

I wanted so much to show off my bride to my family. We got to Rising Star and found my mom remarried and very pregnant. To date, this was her fourth marriage and she had five children fathered by two husbands. The one on the way would be fathered by a third husband.

Everyone was thrilled to meet Bessie and very happy for me. Mom expressed her excitement by feeding us leftovers that evening and taking us to a tent revival that night. My mom got baptized that evening. I wondered how many times that made.

On a visit to the Post Office, I saw my name posted on a list of people deferred from the draft. It read, "Reuben Everett Gotcher, deferred due to age of 98 years." Wow, what a good mistake I had made several months before. The war was coming to an end, so there would be no questions asked.

We had visited for a few days, then decided to go to Odessa. This would give us an opportunity to visit with my father and seek employment. The oil fields were growing and there was also ranch work around the Odessa area.

My dad, Miss Lillie, and the rest of the family were doing great. Dad had bought some land and was raising some sheep, plus buying, selling, and trading any merchandise he ran across.

Dad round us a one-room cabin and we rented it for twelve dollars a month. It had a bed, dining table, stove, and ice box. The water pump was only about twenty feet from the house and the necessary facilities a bit further.

Russell was working in the oilfields and, as soon as we were settled in, I went out with him. This would be a new experience for me. There were probably two men available for every job. Each morning, everyone would arrive early and, about twenty minutes before starting time, a whistle would blow signaling for everyone to line up. A foreman and a timekeeper would walk down the line picking out the men who looked the healthiest and have them step forward. The others were sent home for the day and could come back the next day. A couth, sniffles, bloodshot eyes, or any sign of weakness meant no work and no pay for that day. You could try again tomorrow. They really wanted people who could turn out about eleven hours work in the ten-hour shift. It was sad to see men beg and cry to be allowed to work. You knew they had families and the money had run out.

My brother, Lester, occasionally worked in the oilfields, but had become a really good square dance caller. He could make about as much money on a Friday and Saturday night calling dances as he could make working a week in the oilfields. He was often called to neighboring towns and was well known in the area.

Russell and I were fortunate as we got picked for work each time that we lined up. The only good thing about it was that you weren't absent if you took a day off. However, once you established yourself as being a good worker, they would be asking why you weren't there the previous day.

When springtime rolled around, we had saved a little money and were expecting a blessed event. It was obvious we needed a bigger place and a change of scenery was in order. Bessie had been writing home and the letters coming back suggested that things were healing and that it would be nice if we were to come back that way. I knew Bessie needed to be reunited with her family. Therefore, we set off for Colorado and, hopefully, a happy reunion.

CHAPTER 7

COLORADO AND BEYOND

Bessie's family was thrilled to have her back. Her mother acted like nothing had happened, and brothers, Harrison and Tom, both cried when they saw her. I believe her dad had tears in his eyes. We stayed with them for a few weeks until a baby girl was born. It really hurt that it was a difficult birth and our first daughter, Bessie Evelyn, died within a few hours.

I found work on a ranch near Lamar and we got our own place. In a very short time, Bessie was pregnant again. In August of 1920, a son, Gordon James Gotcher, was born. In June of 1921, another girl, Betty Ruth, was born. Our second son, Robert Harrison, was born in November of 1922.

Knowing that a family the size of ours could not survive with just a motorcycle, we traded it in, along with two hundred fifty dollars, for a 1921 Ford. It was obvious that part-time farm work and a few rodeos wouldn't do well, either.

Diphtheria ravaged the area in 1923 and Betty Ruth contracted the dreaded disease and died at age 2. Though heartbroken, we felt fortunate that God had spared the remainder of our family. Later that year, we moved to Colorado Springs where a trade school was in operation.

For the five years of our marriage, Bessie had been using her teaching knowledge and got me to where my reading and math skills were up to eighth or ninth grade levels. This was above average in this era. For some reason, my handwriting and my ability to construct proper sentences never developed.

I attended a trade school in the evenings in Colorado Springs and quickly developed a knowledge of gas welding. I also took classes in blue print reading. I did well in both areas.

I had been working on a farm and doing the rodeo thing in neighboring towns during rodeo season. With the birth of a daughter, Joan, in 1924, Bessie and I decided that maybe the rodeos should be dropped. We feared that I might get hurt and that we should take advantage of my newly learned welding skills.

Deciding that Texas was the place to go, we packed up and headed for southeastern Texas. We made a brief stop in Rising Star on the way. My mother was still producing children that would be as young as, or younger, than their nephews and nieces. She had boys, L. C., in 1922, and Steve, in 1924. A girl, Fern, was born in 1926. There was 28 years difference in my age and my sister, Fern. Mom was just 44 when Fern was born.

We headed out for the oilfields at Spindletop near Beaumont, Texas. I had hoped to get work doing some welding, but my first job was a roust-a-bout, a kind of general labor, in the Beaumont area. I didn't like the work and, before we really got settled in, we moved to Humble, Texas, northeast of Houston, where the Humble Oil Company was established. I did get to do welding and lay out there and was compensated well for the times.

Texaco offered me work in Texas City in 1928. Because there was a lot of overtime involved, I quickly accepted. This meant moving the family to Galveston, a move that they all accepted and loved.

Galveston had been destroyed by a hurricane in 1900 and between six and seven thousand people had lost their lives. Therefore, a 20-feet seawall had been built and all the buildings and homes were pretty modern.

Swimming and picnics were our primary source of entertainment. Joan, even at age 5, was a good swimmer and showed good athletic ability. Gordon and Bob were both excellent swimmers, but when it came to Bessie, that was something else. Two things she never had got the hang of were swimming and riding a bike. If you asked the children, they would probably add driving a car, even though I thought she did reasonably well at that.

I know that she really regretted not being able to swim, as every mother would like to be in a position to rescue a child, if necessary. But despite holding her by the middle and letting her splash her arms and feet, once released she sank like a rock.

Generally, I was along and, though I never rescued anyone, I was a strong swimmer and could swim for quite a distance. Knowing they worried about me when I would swim out where I could no longer been seen, I would then turn and come back. Those waters often have rip tides and I was lucky to have never got caught in one. Several swimmers drowned each year because of these tides.

CHAPTER 8

THE GREAT DEPRESSION

We were doing pretty well, as was the rest of the country. Everyone was making money and it was the happiest time of the roaring 20's. Then one fateful day in October, 1929, the bottom fell out for everyone. The banks closed, the stock market crashed, and the plants were rapidly closing. My work in Texas City came to an abrupt ending. I got into the bank before it ran out of money and got what little we had saved. We were sorry to learn that the bank president committed suicide later that day.

With a little luck, Chicago Bridge and Iron asked me to oversee the setting of a boiler at a powerhouse in Kansas City. The job would only last a few weeks, but perhaps there would be other work along the Missouri River.

I had a fairly decent old Chevrolet and the 700-mile trip from Galveston to Kansas City took two days. We rented a cabin for one night in Fort Smith, Arkansas. Bessie always liked to stay in cabins. We would have the car right there and they all had cooking facilities, so we could feed our family for a dollar or two. The cabins generally had dishes and pots and pans. In most of them, there was flour and cooking grease, so except for bread, meat, and milk, we would be set.

Throughout the depression, we might have ragged clothes, but they were clean and well patched. Food was always available, though we sure got tired of hamburger steaks. We never had to stay in a tent, but sometimes, the facilities were not much better.

The day after I reported to the jobsite, the boiler we were going to install was arriving. We made arrangements with the Kansas City Local Boilermakers Union for manpower.

We got the boiler set without any problems, but a couple of the guys really began to dog it when we started installing the tubes. It got bad enough that I had to fire two of them because they just wouldn't produce. I ignored the usual threats as the left the jobsite. Generally, we would never see a man again if we fired him. Those we did see would usually try to stay out of sight. This was not the case with these two fellows.

No telephones were available on the jobsite, so I drove down to the Union Hall the next morning to get replacements for the two guys who had been terminated. I talked with the Business Agent and he agreed that these two men were just giving labor a bad name. He said I would have two replacements the following morning.

As I was leaving the hall, one of these guys was loitering outside near the parking lot. He had five of his buddies with him, made a couple of smart remarks, and then charged at me. I knocked him down, let him get up, and then knocked him down again. At this point, his friends entered the contest. Even though I gave it my best, they beat me up pretty good. My face was a real mess. They finally let up and I laid there for a few minutes and then staggered to the car. I drove home, hardly able to see where I was going.

Bessie tried to persuade me to go to the hospital, but other than cuts and bruises, the only other damage was a broken nose which pointed to the side of my face. There really wasn't much that could be done about a broken nose, doctor or no doctor. I took a toothbrush, shoved the handle up the nostril, and this kind of arranged it back in normal order. It hurt like the dickens for the next couple of days, but in later years, very little sign of the breakage could be seen.

We finished in Kansas City in about six weeks and, toward the end, we began to wonder just what the depression had in store for us. Chicago Bridge did not anyplace for me to go. They were going to start building the highest building in New York and would need to hire hundreds of men to work on it. I tried to talk Bessie into us going, but she was totally against it. This was probably a good decision, as they had ten men waiting for every position. I felt that I could do okay as a riveter or welder. Maybe I was lucky that we didn't go. Seven men were killed on that project. Of course, construction standards of the era were such that one man would be killed for every million dollars that the project cost. That was just an accepted fact of life.

CHAPTER 9

NEBRASKA AND NEW MEXICO

We heard that there were a couple of powerhouses being built in the Omaha area, so we started driving up there. It was only about 170 miles and we went there with high hopes.

Disappointment greeted us as work on the powerhouse at Blair, Nebraska, was suspended until additional financing could be arranged.

I wanted to go back to Texas and try the oilfields, but Bessie would have no part of it. She had heard so much about Bonnie and Clyde and did not realize that they also did robberies in nearby states, including Missouri and Nebraska.

We had rented a cabin by the week which was hardly large enough for the five of us, plus our dog, Bill. Our dog was our salvation, or the only income producer we had. He was about as mean as any bulldog you would want to meet. However, with our family, he was our best friend.

Dog fighting was popular in those days, even though many cities, including Omaha, had ordinances against them. A lot of betting went on at a dog fight and Bill was unbeatable. He was low and would attack the opponent's legs, usually breaking one, but always taking the fight out of the other dog. I generally made 20 to

30 dollars a week on bets. Most of these fights were held in a barn or a garage in Omaha, but occasionally, when the police put the heat on, we would cross the river to Council Bluffs, Iowa. We could fight out in the open there, as Iowa did not have laws against dog fights.

One day, Bill got stolen and we thought our meal ticket was gone for good. I drove around looking for him several evenings. The old Chevy made a lot of noise and I guess Bill recognized the sound, because one night, he came running out of a yard. He was dragging a chain and a stake with him. I sure was glad to get him back, but a couple of weeks later, he was taken again and we never did get him back.

We got a letter from my mom that cousin Burl had an auto repair shop in Ozona, New Mexico. He wanted someone to come in and take over the payments which were only sixty dollars a month. This included the purchase of the garage, the used car lot, and all the tools to do the repair work.

Bessie and I were quick in deciding that this was for us and we sent a telegram to Burl saying that we would take it and would be there in about a week. Bessie hated to go through Texas, still fearing Bonnie and Clyde, but that was about the only choice we had. I wanted to see my folks.

After brief visits with my mom, and then to Odessa to see my dad, we were on our way. She said they were saving up a little and planning on moving to California. This would allow her to be near her brothers who had settled in Ontario, near Los Angeles.

On the trip, I gave a lot of thought as to what a great wife and a great bunch of kids I had. Bessie was always ready and willing to pack up and move. The kids had seldom been in the same school for over four months. Still, they stayed out of trouble and got good grades.

Burl hung around for a few days to help me get settled in. Then, he headed for California to join other Porterfield family members.

The shop was awfully busy. We did lots of body and brake work, plus broken drive lines and axels. These were always problems on older cars. Unfortunately, I would get the work done and the car owner would be unable to pay for my services and materials. Some people traded us groceries and clothing to pay their bill. Others just left their vehicles with me, asking me to sell it and split the money with them. However, there were very few buyers then. Really, there wasn't a problem; none of us had anything. The kids had a great time playing in all the old cars and I had time to really fix up a Model A sedan which would become our family car. Everyone was optimistic that things would get better.....A WHOLE LOT BETTER!

I was keeping my ears open for opportunities, as this was not turning out to be the gold mine we needed.

In the summer of 1931, a welding job was offered to me in Borger, Texas. Bessie was very much opposed to us going there. Not only were there gangsters in Texas, but Borger had the worst reputation of any town anywhere. We abandoned the garage and left anyway.

Just before the depression, Borger grew from just a few thousand to over forty-five thousand people. This growth happened almost overnight. Tents, lean to's, and cardboard shacks were the order of the day. With crime and prostitution running wild, the city officials asked the state government for help. They sent the State Police and the Texas Rangers. The unsavory elements were quickly rounded up, but with the jails full, more accommodations were needed.

They stretched a steel cable around the town and shackled the ends together. Then, they took the prisoners and handcuffed one arm to the cable. A judge would come by daily and pronounce sentence, which was usually any money they had. Plus, they had to leave town. They chose to leave town very fast, as authorities were burning down the tent and cardboard city they had been living in. This happened almost two years before we got there, but it was still fresh in everyone's mind, including Bessie's. She sure didn't want to expose the children to that kind of trash.

The oil company used me to do critical welding and to help them train other welders for plant maintenance. I was used more as an instructor and engineer than as a welder. I was one of the very few in the country doing arc welding at this time. This was bare wire welding and it would really burn your arms. Later, flux was put on the welding rod, which allowed you a chance to control the burning splatter.

I needed a helper and Bessie's brother, Harrison, also known as Doc, had come out from Colorado for a visit and I was able to get him employment. Bessie had found a small, three bedroom house with no indoor plumbing, but the price was right. Thus, even with Doc there, we had more room than usual.

The landlord's wife was a stout woman about 50 years young. She wasn't happy having rented the place to Bessie for thirty dollars a month and, when Doc came to stay with us, she wanted an additional five dollars a month. We refused this and she became an inhospitable landlady. She was always complaining about the children and sometimes yelled at them for just being kids. She and Bessie often tangled, but we stayed on, because the size of the house suited our needs.

One evening, Bessie, Doc and I were sitting out on the front porch and we saw her going into the outhouse. Doc said to me, "What do you think, Jack?" I jumped up and said, "Good idea." We ran over to the back side of the facility and tipped it forward so it would turn over with the door facing down.

She screamed and hollered and, when her husband came out, Doc and I, who had returned to the front porch, jumped up to help him. When her husband saw what had happened, he quietly laughed and we all tilted it back up. She looked at Doc and me with that look of, "I know that you did it." Her husband said he'd seen a couple of darkie's run off and thought it must have been them. I guess she accepted this, as she had no real proof of anything else.

We had been in Borger for almost a year when Bessie gave birth to a new baby girl, Phyllis Jean. We now had a perfect-sized family, two girls and two boys. Phyllis was born on May 31st, 1932.

Her birth was three months after the purported kidnapping of the Lindberg baby. With school out and no set bedtime, our son, Bob, armed himself with a BB gun and stood watch over baby Phyllis to keep that old kidnapper away. Bobby was 10 at the time. It must have worked; she wasn't kidnapped.

Shortly after Phyllis's birth, I went to the company doctor complaining about a sore throat that I'd had for some time. He had me lay down on his table. He put an either saturated cloth over my nose and, before I knew it, my tonsils had been removed. He told me to stay home for two days and eat nothing but jello and ice cream during this time. By dinner time that night, I was so starved for solid food, I grabbed a whole pan of cornbread and ate it. I started bleeding real bad and ended up spending two days in the hospital where I definitely stayed on soft foods.

It was late in 1934 and Bessie was feeling much better about living in Texas. First, Borger was no longer the hell hole it had been a couple of years earlier and this was of great importance to her. Bonnie and Clyde had been ambushed in Louisiana and were no longer a threat to anyone.

We didn't really love the Borger area, but it was a living. Many Americans were in bread lines or working WPA projects. Franklin Roosevelt had become President and there was a great change coming over the country. Although I never voted for the man, he had brilliant ideas on getting the country back to financial stability.

A recruiter from the Standard Oil plant in Taft, California, came to see me in the fall. He offered me a lucrative position at the plant in Taft. I would be hired by Chicago Bridge and Iron and loaned to Standard Oil. I would be given a living allowance and the family would be allowed to use all the Standard Oil facilities. These included a gymnasium, indoor swimming pool, and many outdoor sport facilities. It was too good to be true, but they wanted me there in a hurry.

I hated to leave the company in Borger on such short notice, but this was very important to my family. Bessie was pregnant again and we would need more money. With the depression still on, this was a great opportunity which might never happen again.

A few days later, we were ready to leave.

CHAPTER 10

CALIFORNIA, HERE WE COME

With a homemade trailer hitch and a trailer that I traded our sofa for, we loaded up with clothing, and as much of our things as we could, and headed out to California. I drove eighteen to twenty hours a day and Bessie would drive the other four. Though Bessie was not an accomplished driver, her driving certainly was better than her swimming or bike riding. Alternating driving on the trip seemed to work all right.

Somewhere around Winslow, Arizona, the trailer came off and we didn't even notice it. As we had no idea where it had come off, there was no need to turn around and go back looking for it. Route 66 was two lanes all the way and, when we hit the western Arizona and eastern California deserts, there were many vehicles by the side of the road due to overheating. We knew that one must never pass a service station without getting gas, because the next station may be 250 miles away. This was late 1934 and air conditioning on card was unheard of. We were fortunate that it was late fall. I would hate to have to drive it in the summer when the temperatures would reach 120 degrees or more.

We were blessed; we made it to Taft without incidence. The Model A ran very well. I had been able to keep it in good condition with the mechanical knowledge I had begun learning since childhood.

Bessie went house hunting and round a decent place in the Ford City section of Taft. Finding one, particularly one that was furnished, was no easy task. There were tent cities throughout California. These were the days that unscrupulous labor brokers were spreading leaflets throughout Texas, Oklahoma, and Arkansas. The leaflets read, "High paying agricultural work available in California." People would pack, load up, and make their way as best they could. Upon arrival, they were finding no housing and, worst of all, no jobs, as they were 10 deep in line. John Steinbeck's book, "The Grapes of Wrath", did an excellent job of describing the situation. The saying, "Hey Okie, if you see Arkie, tell him I'm on my way to Califor-nee-a just to pick prunes." There was no minimum wage law and most work was piece work, so much per box or bag. Children as young as four or five were working all day in the fields to put a few pennies on the table.

On January 17th, 1935, only a couple of months after arriving in Taft, Bessie gave birth to a son, a healthy nine pound baby boy. Bob would not have to sit up all night with his BB gun. On that same day, Richard Hauptmann was convicted and sentenced to die for killing the Lindberg baby.

We argued over the years whether his name was Michael Don or Mickey Don. I felt it was Mickey, as I filled out the birth certificate. Bessie held out that it was Michael. It was years later that we learned it was Michael. He still always went by Mickey. I don't know why I thought I had put Mickey on the birth certificate.

My mother had finally moved to the Los Angeles area and was very excited about it. Revivals everywhere. She had gone to one for a week leaving L. C., Steve, and Fern pretty much unsupervised. L. C., now 13, found a whiskey bottle and thought it was whiskey. It was filled with coal oil. L. C., not having any previous drinking experience, took several swallows despite the bad taste. He died within a few hours. Mom got back home the day after he died and sent us a telegram. I drove down for the funeral. Bessie, with the new baby, was unable to go with me.

The job with Standard Oil Company was great. It consisted partly of meeting with engineers and planning the work and, at other times, personally doing or supervising all code welding in this large refinery.

My cousin, Omie Porterfield Albritton, moved from Ontario, California, to Taft when I was able to get her husband, Lee, a position with Standard Oil. Lee was a pretty good welder and would contribute a lot to Standard's needs. Omie would be an absolute blessing in helping care for Bessie and baby Mickey. The Albrittons had three children. Exa, who was the same age as Gordon; Raymond, who was the same age as Bob; and Harry, who was the same age as our daughter, Joan. It was good for the kids to have relatives and friends.

My son, Bob, and Raymond were the wild ones. They were teenagers and very mischievous. Neither family could keep butter in the ice box. I do mean ice box, an insulated box where a block of ice was placed in the top section to keep food cool. Bob and Raymond would take the butter, climb under the kitchen table, and eat a pound or two at one setting. We punished them several times to no effect. Whether it was something they just wanted to try to get away with, or a drug-like craving, I'll never know.

We had been in Taft for only about six months when I was invited to attend a planning meeting with the senior partners in the formation of the Arabian American Oil Company, later to be known as ARAMCO. I was introduced to Les White, a well-regarded senior engineer for Standard Oil. The meeting was fast and to the point. They would like Les and me to go to Saudi Arabia and get some of the construction activities started. Drilling teams were in place and having great luck, though they were having to cap off all their finds. There was no way to move the oil or any place to store or transport it. We were going to need some pipelines, storage tanks, loading docks, and other necessities. It would be Les's and my responsibility to be over some of this work. The other partners involved would have similar teams working on some of these projects. They wanted to be selling large volumes of oil within a year!

It would be hard to leave home, but it was going to be four hundred dollars per month, tax free, and a one thousand dollar bonus for completing the project. Bessie and I discussed and it was decided that this was the way to go.

About that time, cousin Burl came up to visit us. He had brought his dad's new roadster and, when we told him we were going to need to make a trip to Los Angeles to see my mom before I left for Saudi, he insisted on going with us and taking the roadster. Bessie was still under the weather and it was decided that, along with Burl, that Gordon, Bob, and Joan would go down with us. From Taft, it would be 130 miles to Los Angeles going to Bakersfield to pick up Highway 99.

In those days, a trip to Bakersfield to Los Angeles would be the talk of the neighborhood for several days. It was a two-lane, winding road with a few mountain passes to navigate. They called it the Grapevine, as it wound and went up and down like branches on a grape vine. It also led to some rich, agricultural areas where grapes were grown. There were always cars beside the road that had overheated climbing the mountains. After making such a trip, a person was almost obligated to go to the barber shop, so they could tell and retell what was encountered on the way. You would have to repeat your tale to many other individuals. Some would say, "I'm going to make that trip next year and I was wondering what to expect." They certainly weren't Gotchers. Planning a 130-mile trip in advance? No way!

We took off and I was the one to drive over the grapevine, as Burl said he would rather not. We were behind a Coca Cola truck going over one particularly steep and winding portion, having to slow down and drive in low gear, as the truck could hardly move. I let Gordon climb out on the hood and I pulled up to where I was almost touching the truck. Gordon removed five bottles of Coke and we all enjoyed hot Coca Cola. In later years, I would have been arrested for child endangerment.

We got to mom's house to find her gone to a church function in the San Fernando Valley. My brother, Steve, and sister, Fern, were very ill. Immediately, I got a doctor to make a house call and he had us take them to a hospital for a stomach pump.

Mom had left them for several days with little or no food. They had chickens in the back yard, so Steve and Fern caught a couple, killed them, and picked the feathers off as best they could. They then put them in a pot and boiled them until done. They had not cleaned the chickens and both had become deathly ill from the little eating they had done. Throughout the remainder of their lives, neither one would ever eat chicken in any form.

My mom was such a good person and all of us loved her to no end. However, she sometimes would neglect the family to pursue the Lord's work. She strongly believed that the Lord would take care of everything. That is how she lived with the loss of L. C., and the near loss of Steve and Fern. These were not isolated events, but more of a pattern. She would not change, but on her behalf, she was such a loving and giving person.

We had a nice visit, though Bob and Joy were unhappy, as Steve and Fern were not well enough to play. Our trip back to Taft was uneventful.

A sad event occurred just prior to my leaving. In those days, theatre marquees were used to update the news and important events throughout the day. Driving through downtown Taft, there was a message on the marquee of the theater that read: **WILL ROGERS AND WILEY POST KILLED IN ALASKA PLANE CRASH"**

Though I never got to see him, some of the rope tricks and things that I was able to perform made people compare me to him. I always enjoyed his humor and his political views. Oklahoma had made him their favorite-son candidate for President of the United States in 1932. He laughed it off, but I really think that he would have made a very good one. He sure would have been for the working man.

Shortly before my departure, I got a big surprise. First, Bessie's mother showed up with her brother, Tom James. Then later on the same day, my mom showed up with my sisters, Jan and Fern, and brother, Steve. My cousin Burl arrived that evening. Of course, Lee and Omie and their three were there. We decided to have a long weekend stay together. It was easy to put up a bunch of people then. Pallets were set up in the living room and the kids, all nine of them, were sent to sleep on the screened porch. We played a card game called Rook. It was the only card game that Bessie would allow, as anything else would be gambling. It was really a great weekend.

The time for my departure was at hand. This would be the first time that we could not just pick up, pack, and take the whole family. I sure did not like it, but Bessie and I agreed that it was really something we needed to do. This was our chance to find that pot of gold.

CHAPTER 11

FAR FROM HOME

Standard Oil furnished a driver and a station wagon to take Les White and me to the train station at Bakersfield. We both had four trunks and a couple of suitcases. Two of my trunks were filled with tools, a welding hood, gloves, and various instruments used in construction. The other two had work clothes. I would be wearing my suit and Stetson. I believe that Les had similar items, though he was also carrying drawings and planning materials. We would change trains in Los Angeles, and again in St. Louis, on our four and a half days trip to New York City. I was amazed at the size of New York and, when seeing the Empire State Building, even from a distance, I was glad I hadn't worked on it. It was almost a quarter of a mile high.

Les and I could not figure why it was cheaper for the oil company to have us spend seven weeks going by train, then by boat, to Saudi Arabia, when we could have flown across the U. S. in 10 hours and on to Europe in another 12 or 15 hours. That would have left us with only about three weeks on a ship. They at least would have cut our non-productive time in half. Of course, neither of us knew what it cost to take the Pan American Clipper across the Atlantic.

We had been led to believe that the climate on the east coast of Saudi Arabia would be hot, very similar to Taft, but we found it to be much hotter. It was a very primitive country. Brick and adobe buildings were going up, but many of the Arabs wanting to retain their old ways preferred to live in tents. It was not uncommon to see a sheik living in a tent with a Rolls Royce parked in front.

The Saudi's were awakened each morning by the call of the priest for prayer. This came each morning around 5:00 a.m. Everyone, but babies and sick people, was required to participate. They would pray a total of seven times a day.

They were quite protective of their women, not allowing them to be seen without being totally covered from head to toe. No picture taking of the women was allowed.

Mohammed had once described them as being "beast of burden and like the jackals of the desert, born without soul." This came about when one of Mohammad's young wives had an expensive bracelet disappear. It was found in the tent of a male friend of the great warrior and religious leader. From that day, some 1,200 years earlier to the present, women's rights were non-existent.

King Ibn Saud, in the year 1900, had organized the tribes and had driven the British out of Arabia. He divided the country into four sections, setting up a close relative to be the Amir (governor) in each area. He forbade the tribes to be nomads, forcing them to live either along the coastline or at an oasis. They still would have rather fought each other than co-exist peacefully. To gain some unification, he married a woman from each tribe, often divorcing one a few hours after marriage, to stay within the guidelines of the Koran, the Muslim bible. In this manner, each tribe was able to feel special, as they had some royalty in their tribe.

He tried to visit each tribe on a monthly basis to hear their complaints or problems and conduct trials, if there were any criminal charges pending.

One such case involved a woman who wanted a man put to death for murdering her husband. The king asked what had happened and she said that her husband, Ali, had gone with his friend, Salah, to pick dates. Her Ali had gotten awfully tired from the walk and lay down under the date tree. Salah climbed up the tree to pick dates, fell out of the tree on top of Ali, and murdered him. The king, wanting to be fair, but bound by the law of the Koran, asked her if she would take four thousand dollars in blood money rather than have Salah killed. She said, "No, the money will just be gone and will not replace Ali." He then asked her and Salah to accompany him to the tree where the murder took place. He then said, "Salah, you lay down exactly as Ali was." Salah did this. He instructed the women to climb the tree, fall on Salah, and murder him the way he had murdered Ali. She changed her mind and took the blood money.

King Saud would occasionally ride along the desert and, if he saw smoke, would stop and have Chi (tea) with whoever had the fire going. The story goes that whoever he had Chi with was given a Rolex watch on departure. True or not, this helped keep them close to roadways and stopped the Nomads from returning to the really barren desert.

Les told me a couple of stories that he learned at some staff meetings. One was of a small village that was going to punish a resident for a sex crime. The Koran said the punishment was for the offender to be put in a sack and thrown from the highest building in town. Their town representative went to the oil company and asked if they could use the company's airplane. He said they were a poor town and had no tall buildings. The request was denied and we often wondered how they handled the situation.

The Saudi's were always swift and harsh in carrying out punishment.

Punishment day was Friday's and everyone would be rounded up and forced to witness any punishment scheduled for that day. Punishments ranged from flogging to beheading. I was once forced to witness them cutting off a man's hand for stealing. Though beheadings were common, I was lucky not to be out in public when any of these were carried out. Therefore, I was not rounded up with the crowd.

Les and I began building storage tanks and running oil lines to a gathering center in the desert. A jetty, or dock, was being built near

Dammam where the tankers would load. Refining facilities were being started at a desert outpost called Abqaiq, and one was in the planning stage along the coast north of Dammam.

The job was going pretty well. Our help had been recruited from the United Kingdom and they were an average bunch of guys. No liquor was available, so we had no problems along those lines.

I had been there for 10 months when Les called me in and said that they had directed that he finish the job alone. I was to report back to Taft. He said they were going to reassign me to Ceylon, Colombo, India. It is now known as Sri Lanka. I wasn't excited about being told where I was going, but I felt that if you worked for someone, you did what they wanted you to do.

Besides, I was quite excited to be going home. I would get home as fast as a letter, so there was no need to write ahead that I was coming. I could send a telegram when the ship got to New York. I was now ready for my six week adventure at sea.

The train from New York took five days and I took a taxi from Bakersfield to Taft. It cost three dollars for the 38-mile trip.

CHAPTER 12

HOME, THEN OFF TO INDIA

It is ironic that I had traveled over six weeks to be home for six weeks, then off to Ceylon, Colombo. This was a trip that would take about seven weeks, but that was the way of things in 1936.

I found the family to be well and enjoying the Standard Oil prestige. In Taft at this time, people working for Standard Oil were the elite of the community and the use of the facilities was super, particularly the indoor swimming pool.

However, as the family was still living in Ford City, it was too far off to go, other than to be driven. I bought Bessie a new 1936 Pontiac coupe for six hundred forty dollars. I also took Gordon down to get a driver's license. He was now 16 and had been driving since he was 11.

I had brought gifts for everyone. I had silk dresses and feminine scarves for my ladies. The boys got several two-sided curved Arabian knives in fancy decorated scabbards with semi-precious stones on the cases. They all seemed happy with the gifts. Phyllis was four and Mickey, one, so their gifts were locally purchased toys.

Bessie and I vowed that we would move to Taft Heights on my return. It was a nicer area of Taft and was within bike riding range of the Standard Oil gym and swimming pool. This would be a big help in keeping Gordon, age 16, Bob, now age 14, and Joy, now age 12, occupied. I had my doubts if Bessie would see much of the Pontiac now that Gordon had a license.

The visit was all too short. We had a couple of family picnics, but did not find time to make the trip to Los Angeles where most of my kin were living.

Bob Tucker, a Standard Oil engineer, was assigned to the Ceylon project. It was obvious that he was not another Les White. Les had always done his work and had a lot of fun in doing it. Bob didn't really seem to be too interested in the job, figuring that all the planning was done and the engineering was complete. That left a lot more responsibility on me. It was not that I minded, but I had my hands full figuring out the equipment we would need and going through the process of getting it ordered through a Ceylon broker. I was not yet familiar with India and didn't realize that the biggest piece of equipment would be an elephant.

Bessie drove me to the train depot in Bakersfield. Bob Tucker was already there, coming up with a driver in the new suburban that Standard Oil had purchased. They had checked in our luggage, except for the two suitcases I would carry with me. These contained the clothing I would need for the seven week trip.

Bessie and I hugged and talked of remembering dreams, which included a move to Taft Heights and later on to a big ranch somewhere in the west. She said that she didn't care where the ranch was, as long as it wasn't Texas.

We boarded the Southern Pacific Southbound and changed to the Eastbound in Los Angeles. Somewhere on our way to New York, it became the Santa Fe Super Chief, but I believe that was only an engine switch. We did not change trains again.

The ship we were on took us to Egypt and we spent almost a week waiting for the ship that would take us to Ceylon. After that delay and a couple of other stops, it had been nine weeks from the time we left Taft until our arrival in India.

We were to build and pipe up 26 oil storage tanks which were capable of holding 200,000 barrels of oil each, and they needed them fast.

Our work crews were made up mostly of Indian boys, but we had several British welders and a couple of foremen who were Brits. This was a different atmosphere from Saudi. Booze was plentiful and the British do drink. There were several times I wanted to fire all of them and I would have, but upper management would not allow it. They felt it would take six to eight weeks to replace them and the replacements would probably be no better than the ones we fired. This was probably quite true.

Mail was infrequent, usually taking eight weeks each way. Phones were not available and would not have been of any use to me, anyway, since we didn't have one at home. We could send telegrams to the home office if we needed clarification on engineering details.

Tucker and I did a lot of talking in the evenings, in lieu of entertainment. He became interested in my ranching plans and asked if he could get in as a partner when the time came. Figuring that the more money that was invested, the more money would be made, I said yes. It was a long way off and, if he opted out, so be it.

The world was waiting for the Max Schmeling, Joe Lewis fight. I bet pretty heavily on Schmeling using the logic, "No black man can beat a good white man." Lewis changed a lot of minds. When I made my statement, I had forgotten about Jack Johnson, a Galveston black, holding the heavyweight title for several years until Jess Willard took it away from him in 1914. Prejudice seems to dim the memory of another race's accomplishments. I lost one hundred dollars, which I didn't dare tell Bessie about.

On the project, elephants were used in place of cranes. I learned a lot about handling them from the natives. They were smart, obedient, and good at pulling pipe and making heavy lifts. They could lift equipment up weighing over a ton and move it to the required place. On repetitive functions, you could almost leave them all day and they would keep performing. Each elephant had its own special handler. These guys washed the elephants daily and kept them close to a water hole at night. The handler usually slept outside with their elephants.

The caste system is an accepted practice in India and we had to be very careful with the placement of workers. If perhaps you moved a man of lower caste into a crew with higher caste workers, there would be a fight before the days end. We had four or five central gathering points where workers were picked up and bussed into work. The local police patrolled these areas so that everyone was allowed on the bus. At the end of the day, I had a big Indian male who carried a baseball bat and walked around the bus to see that everyone was given entry. He would use the bat once or twice a week. We were lucky inasmuch as no knifings occurred on the jobsite, but we did lose some workers due to knifings in town. They all carried switchblades.

Entertainment was almost non-existent. There were bars and sporting houses, but no one from our culture would touch any of the whores. The British boys drank a lot and played darts. We couldn't find anyone interested in singing and fiddling because the British and American cultures clashed when it came to music.

I was fair at darts and occasionally played darts with the Brits. I generally broke even. Even when I lost, it was just loose change or drinks, so no money really changed hands. I did get a few of them interested in Poker and, though they learned the game fairly well, their drinking made them a made them a bit easy to beat at the game.

The work was going along pretty well, though my work crews were somewhat undependable. The British, with their drinking problems, and the Indians, with their caste system, caused issues. Still, we were pretty much on schedule.

The following was a letter written to Bessie in 1937. (Writer's Note: Though rewritten for clarity, the verbiage and spelling remains the same. I still had not mastered my writing and spelling skills. I never would.)

Ceylon Colombo

Dearest Onee,

Just received the letter with the small pictures in it. How ever the large pictures, even though mailed later had been here about 2 weeks. aren't they dear? Sure wish I could hold them in person. I supose you are recouprating or what ever it is from the 4th of July. The company shut down every where but here. But I didn't. the 4th is just another day to the natives and british, well it is just another day and I got a lot of work done. I let the welders off and they got drunk and had a fight in the Hotel so they were put in jail for a night. This morning they fined them and let them out. They got to work about 10:30A.M. I wanted to fire them but I didn't would take 6 weeks to get more and they might be just as bad. Dear it is to had about Mr. Case dieting but I was like you I have been half way expecting it. They just can't forget you no and they just sit around the house and broad over the loss of their companion and at that age their nerves won't stan it. I know just going away to work is tough enough. I have easily age 10 yeas the past few months and have had my mind absolutley occupied all the time. the job is getting well underway. I am putting the 3rd ring on 1 tank, the second ring on another and the first pipelines left for the welders. but the floating rooms will take a long time you no. This is like what I did in Texas City you no. I am afraid we will be here several more months getting through. So LeeAlbritton went to Boulder Dam. Must be some good money there as he had a good deal going with Standard oil. What does Omie think of that? I would have liked to have seen

75

the dam under construction but doubt if I would care about seeing it finsihed and of course I saw it fromte air. the plane circled it very low and slow. ut after all you still could hardly see it. To bad you won't get to see Bernice this summer. why don't you drive down to where she live it wont cost you much and I don't mind. I want ring finished on another and starting a first ring on another tank tomorrow. I have all the bottoms welded now. just the roofs and you to see your old friends. and I like Clyde and Bernice both. I to never thought any woman would part me from some of my friend, old Harvey McKee for instance. But here I am and going strong only I am about to starve to death for some right food but you can go see them all. I mean your friends that you want to see. I think it is very nice of the Browns to be so nice to the babbys. but don't whip little mick mick for running off whe browns heps him in fact I wouldn't whip him anyway. They wont be babbyes butg once. I wish while you are gabbing picatures you would grab off one of the Pontiac. I would like to show it to my guest here. have showed the babbyes pictures herein the hotel and everyone just have spells about I them. they say they look just like movie stars and Shirley Temple hasn't anything on them and of course I agree with them. you are doing fine putting 800 miles per month but it is yours my dear. Put them on. I just had 2 corns taken off tonight. They are between my toes and you no. It has always hurt me so much you no and lately it has been horrable, well it is gone now. A native took it off. he spedialises in corns and took it off by the roots in 15 minutes almost painless. I wish I had your feet along I could get them fixed too. Well it is 10PM

Love Dad

By the end of the contract, I was about eleven hundred dollars ahead in gambling winnings, so I decided to buy presents for the family with it. In an Indian bazaar, I saw a necklace which was 25 karats with mixed diamonds and sapphires. It had five one karat diamonds and several smaller ones, plus a whole bunch of sapphires. The merchant asked me for the equivalent of twenty-five hundred dollars in rupees. I negotiated with him and finally got him down to fifteen hundred dollars, but would not buy it at that price. I returned to the bazaar a few days later and went into a competitor's shop across the street. I browsed around quite a while, finally bought a cheap little item, and had it wrapped. I knew the first merchant was watching from his shop.

As I left the store, he was in front of his store yelling, "Mister, please come here, please Mister." I told him that I didn't have time and left. I waited a couple of days and, while walking on the other side of the street, I heard him yell, "Mister, Mister!" I walked over and bought the necklace for one thousand dollars.

Hand carved ivory was very cheap and I bought a lot of elephant bracelets and necklaces for the girls. I bought seven or eight elephant tusks for the boys. They played with them a bit and did not gore anyone.

It was getting close to time to return home. I was ready and really happy about it.

CHAPTER 13

BACK TO CALIFORNIA

The job was completed a couple of weeks behind schedule, mostly due to the labor problems that we had with the Brits and the Indians. But at least it was finished and time to go home again. As much as I hated the lost time in sailing, I was sure looking forward to this trip.

It took 46 days to sail from India to New York. Thank goodness for the Suez Canal. If we had been made to sail around Africa, it might have taken us a year. Once again after arriving in New York, we were back on the train headed for Los Angeles, and then Bakersfield.

I sent Bessie a telegram to expect me in six or seven days. As very few people had phones in those days, once the telegram hit the town, it was sent to a messenger who would attempt delivery at first convenience, usually the following day. Mail in the U. S. was usually delivered within a week. I think first-class stamps were two cents then.

When we finally got to Bakersfield, we took a cab. The fare had gone up from three dollars to three dollars fifty cents, so it was one dollar seventy-five cents each. This could go on our expense report. We left our trunks at the railroad station knowing that the company would send a driver to pick them up.

It appeared that there was no one home when I entered the house. Then I heard some baby chatter from one of the bedrooms.

Peeking in, I saw baby Mickey laying there entertaining himself. I talked to him a bit and told him that I was his daddy, but he wouldn't have anything to do with me.

I found Bessie a couple of houses away visiting with neighbors. This got us off on the wrong foot, as I scolded her for leaving that baby alone. She was very cold for several days. I loved my wife and family dearly, but Bessie could turn affection on and off and, after being gone for nearly a year, I really didn't need for it to be turned off.

A few day later, my trunks arrived and I started passing out gifts. The boys liked the ivory tusks and the girls were delighted with their hand carved ivory necklaces and bracelets. Once Bessie got the diamond and sapphire necklace, the cold war was over.

Mickey called me "that man" for a few days, then started calling me Jack instead of daddy. He said, "That man calls me Mickey, so I call him, Jack." It took a few days, but before long he was a daddy's boy. Phyllis was always a daddy's girl.

Mickey had never had a haircut and Bessie and I argued about it. He had long beautiful curls, but I didn't want my boy looking like a girl. I took him to a barber shop. Bessie was crying as we left and Mickey cried in the barber's chair, as he had never been through this before.

Bessie was still driving the Pontiac coupe and it was pretty crowded for our family. We talked of giving Gordon the coupe when he graduated from junior college and buying ourselves a four-door sedan.

I reported to Standard Oil on the first Monday and was not given any particular assignment. I was to help out wherever I could. A great number of the Taft employees were getting ready to go to Saudi and kick that off in a big way. They put me Personnel for about a month to answer questions about what to expect in Saudi. Although I always liked to talk, I thought for a man to be working inside was rather sissified. I got back in the welding shop as soon as I could.

I had not been around Taft enough to really get to know it and this time, I got to learn about my town.

Taft was a very bigoted town. The Ford City section where we were living was mixed racially. There were more children than you ever saw. However, the blacks only played with blacks and whites with whites. It was enjoyable to sit on the porch and watch the children playing with homemade toys. Wagons and scooters, all homemade, were the most popular things. It seemed that each evening the kids figured out a way to line up a parade of some kind.

Something the kids all dreamed of was winning the National Soap Box Derby. They used cars made of wood and wagon wheels which were supposed to be made by a boy and his dad. They would race them down a hill. The winner would go to the regionals, then to state and on to nationals if you kept winning. I believe the grand prize was a two hundred fifty dollar college scholarship. I made a couple of these for son, Bob, but we never got above second place.

The Gotcher's were among the elite, as we had a screened in porch and also a swamp cooler. This made us much better off than our neighbors who had neither. Bessie was getting more insistent that we move from Ford City to Taft Heights, and I told her to go ahead and find a place.

Taft Heights was strictly restricted for the white race. At the time, the Klan was very active in Taft, which was considered by some to be their West Coast headquarters. There were signs on both ends of town which read, "N_____, don't let the sun set on you in this town."

We went to the movies often, especially to see Shirley Temple and Mickey Rooney shows. The entire family loved western movies and Hopalong Cassidy movies were our favorites. A cheap grade B western movie could be turned out in about two weeks, so at least once a month, we got Hopalong shows. He was our favorite, but there were many grade B westerns being produced. We loved all of them. Tarzan was getting to be quite popular, too.

The movie projector would be set up on a table at the rear center of the theater. There would be two reels, so after the first one played, there would be an intermission while they rewound the first reel and set the second on in place. The lights would go on and the concession stands would be staffed.

The local police would make themselves visible and announce, "Now, you colored boys go on home. You know that if you are out after dark, you'll be stealing things and getting in trouble." When this was announced, the blacks, who were restricted to sitting in the back two rows, would get up and leave.

Bessie had looked at a few places in Taft Heights and got me to go look at a place. We both agreed that it was perfect. I went down to talk with the bankers and Bessie did some investigating in the neighborhood. She found that there was a Catholic family living next door. That helped make her decision. She was not going to have her children living next to those heathens. If it had not been Catholics, it would have been Italians, Mexicans, or what have you. I guess maybe she tried to put herself above others because of her name, Bessie James. She had been born in Missouri near where Jesse James had been killed. I'm sure that, as a child, people thought she was related to the infamous bandit.

Shortly before our move to Taft Heights, I noticed Phyllis, age 5, and Mickey, age 3, walking with arms locked around each other's shoulder. They were chanting, "We're moving to Taft Heights and can't no N_____'s live there." It was the way things were then, but I stopped them, at least while I was around. I believe I was more of a separatist than a racist. I hope there is a difference.

We finally found an area where the entire block was Protestants. There were two houses for sale, side by side, with one being on a corner lot. We bought both of them and Bessie's fears of bad neighbors ended.

Both houses were nice, had screened porches, and each had a swamp cooler. I wanted to add a second cooler to the house we were going to live in, but Bessie would have no part of that. Our electric bill was already almost four dollars a month and another cooler would add to that. She was getting an Easy washing machine, one that had rollers on top. After the water was drained, you could wring the laundry out with the rollers before hanging it on the clothesline. I bought a Philco Trans American console radio with an AM band, plus three short waves bands. We were all set now except for one other item. We would have to buy an entire house full of furniture. With a living room set, four bedroom sets, and some porch furniture, it cost us almost three hundred fifty dollars.

Gordon would have no part of the Pontiac coupe and we ended up buying him a 1938 Oldsmobile sedan. It cost right at seven hundred dollars. It was discounted one hundred dollars because the 1939 models were coming out.

I knew that, as a family, we needed something larger than the Pontiac. I made a deal where, if I would go to Detroit and pick up a new Dodge and Plymouth, they would give me a substantial trade-in on the Pontiac. I got Bob Tucker to go to Detroit with me to pick up the cars. We paid five hundred ninety-five dollars for the new Plymouth and six hundred ninety-five for the Dodge. I was given three hundred fifty dollars for my Pontiac. So, for about nine hundred forty dollars, we had two brand new automobiles.

In those days, a Dodge was considered a man's car, so that was mine and Bessie got the Plymouth.

Now that we lived closer to the Standard Oil facility, the family spent a lot more time in the swimming pool. Bessie was still unable to swim, but both Mickey and Phyllis were catching on.

Both the older boys were involved in boxing and Gordon won the Golden Gloves award in his weight class. Bob didn't like to get hit and really didn't do very well. He would look okay in working out, but in a real match, he would cover his face and try not to get hit. He had become a talented metal worker and made his own set of golden gloves. He swore then, and in later years, that he had won them.

Joan was doing well in school and was an outstanding softball player. At age 15, she played on the traveling women's team in Taft and was one of their very best players.

Picnics were a family activity we enjoyed together. One Sunday after church, we talked about maybe having a family picnic that afternoon. There had been some rain in the morning, and there would probably be a few mushrooms to pick out on the desert. Cousin Lee and Omie were going to bring their families, too. It was decided that Bessie and Omie would fry some chicken, make some biscuits and salad, and meet the rest of us as soon as they were done. Lee and I left with their three kids and our five and went on out. A couple of hours later, Bessie and Omie arrived with enough food to feed and army and we had a nice lunch.

After eating, most of us sat around and Gordon went for walk. Phyllis tagged along. She got tired quickly, so he sent her back. He was tall enough that he could see above the sage brush and knew exactly where we were. She was short and, in the fifty yards back to us, she got lost and wandered off in another direction. Gordon returned, noticed she was not with us, and the alarm went out.

We had done so much walking prior to lunch that the sand had tracks all over and we couldn't pick up a trail. Bessie stayed at the picnic site with Mickey and the rest of us began to search. After two hours and no results, we sent Gordon into town to get the Sheriff's Department involved. They showed up with a half dozen town people and the search continued. As it can get pretty chilly at night there and there is always the danger of a rattlesnake, all of us were getting scared.

Just before dark, someone yelled, "She's over here." I ran to my baby girl and all of us knew we had dodged a bullet. A prayer had been answered.

I got Gordon on with Standard Oil as a bookkeeper. I had hoped to teach him some mechanical things, but he did not care to do anything to get dirty. I guess because he was the oldest and was bright, Bessie and I always favored him. I'm sure the others were aware of this. Though unintentional on our part, it was a fact of life.

Bob would work hard at anything except school books. He was interested in the things I did and he did get passing grades, barely. Joan was very bright and got good grades without trying. Despite her small size, she was very athletic and tough. She would have loved to be on the boxing team if they would have let her. I would have bet on her in her weight class.

We were quite surprised when one day my brother, Les Gotcher, showed up at the house. Les had recently won the award as World Champion Square Dance Caller. This was at the 1939 World's Fair in Chicago. He had then signed a contract with RKO, a major motion picture company, and was teaching square dancing to movie stars. He was the background square dance caller in many movies for the next 20 years. Les did a smart thing. He incorporated as, "Les Gotcher, World Champion Square Dance Caller". He kept this title permanently, as no one else could claim the title without infringing on his corporation rights. We had a nice visit before he returned to Hollywood.

Mickey was having a lot of sore throats and we finally took him to have his tonsils removed. In those days, this was done right in the doctor's office. A gauze soaked in ether was placed over the mouth and nose. As soon as he went to sleep, the tonsils were snipped out and we were on our way home. Of course, we were cautioned by the doctor to keep him on liquids for two days.

On the way home that day, the theater marquee had a grim reminder. "Four years ago today, Will Roger and Wiley Post killed in Alaska plane crash." It had been four years and he was still missed and greatly admired.

Mickey slept most of the afternoon, woke up hungry, and wanted toast. He was told that the doctor had told us liquids only for two days. His answer to that was, "Dr. Dykes told me that toast is a liquid." Somehow, we did not believe our four-year old. We remembered the events when I had my tonsils out and we stuck to the rules.

Standard Oil wasn't in a position to let me work full time, so I took a leave of absence. I went over to Boulder Dam in Nevada where a good deal of overtime was being worked. I was hired by Bechtel, Price & Callahan to do inspection of welding. This would help build up the kitty for that ranch. However, it was tough working near Las Vegas. We worked six days a week and it was too far to drive home. One just couldn't make the trip on a one day weekend. The money was good, though, and the job would only last about three months. I hung on to it.

Spring came, the work was completed, and it was time to move on. I was quite anxious to get back with my family and make our next plans.

CHAPTER 14

CHASE THAT RAINBOW

I had been in contact with Bob Tucker during this period and he was still very anxious to get on with our ranching plans. We discussed to great lengths what we would raise and decided to wait until I purchased the land to make a final decision. We would then know approximately the size herd. I figured we could get one sheep per acre and not have to feed them. With cattle, it would be one cow per five acres, and they would still require some winter feed.

With school out, Bessie, Joan, Phyllis, and Mickey were loaded into the Dodge and we headed for northern California and Oregon. We kind of mixed our land search with a vacation and toured the California wine country, the majestic Redwood forests, and the Oregon coast. Some of the roads we traveled in northern California and Oregon were quite scary. In some places, there were one lane roads looking down the sides of mountains. If you were going down and met another car, it was your responsibility to back up to a spot where there was sufficient room for the car traveling uphill to get by. Though I was never put in that situation, I always wondered what would happen if you got all the way to the top and there was still no room to go on. Would you start backing down the other side, and at what point did it become the other driver's job to back up? It seemed like you might be involved in this predicament forever.

There was a lot of rain and we got stuck several times. However, there was a bright spot to this. Following the rain, there were usually rainbows and one was sure to point us to our pot of gold. The constant rain in Oregon made us eliminate that state and center our search in the foothills of northern California. It rained a lot there, too, but not like in Oregon. After a lot of looking, we narrowed our search down to two locations.

One was on the outskirts of Sacramento. We could buy 500 acres for forty dollars per acre. The land ranged from flat to some rolling meadows. It was in the little town of Carmichael.

The other land was located on Highway 49 between Auburn and Grass Valley, 1,709 acres. The price was nine dollars per acre. It was located in the foothills, lots of pine trees and grass. Fifteen hundred acres were on the east side of the road and about two hundred on the west side. It had a perimeter fence all the way around it and a couple of small fenced corrals. There was also a one room cabin and the burned out remains of the old Donner Hotel. Survivors of the Donner party had passed that way, after rescue, on their way to Sacramento.

After a lot of thought, we decided on the larger parcel. We would still be about 998,000 acres shy of being the size of the King Ranch, but this was a start.

The Bank of America owned this land and, for a small down payment, I was given an option to buy the land within 90 days. Will Brundage, the bank president, and I shook hands and I hurried off to get organized. I wanted this place rocking before the first of the year.

Bob and I still had not decided on the makeup of a herd, but I knew darned well that we would need horses. I dropped the family off in Taft and headed for New Mexico. I knew I could buy some horses there from an Indian rancher. I bought six horses and a pony, complete with saddles and bridles, for four hundred dollars. This would include shipping them to me in northern California. I was pleased at the progress that had been made in the past two weeks.

I went back to Taft and had a long sit down with Tucker. Cattle would be stronger, but would require winter feed or range. Sheep would take care of themselves. Cattle would be hard to round up and sheep pretty well stay in herds and follow the leader. The decider, I guess, was that my dad was being very successful in raising sheep in Texas and he would give us a very good price. It was a done deal. I would arrange for him to ship us 2,000 head of sheep.

Bessie found renters for the two houses in Taft. It was early November when I ordered the horses to be sent to Auburn. We loaded up and headed for northern California.

CHAPTER 15

THE WOOL OVER MY EYES

The only place we could find to rent that was close to the ranch was on the Nevada County line just past Bear River. It was a large, three bedroom home. However, it lacked electricity and indoor plumbing. We had lived this way before and would make do until at least spring. The kids were somewhat shocked by it because the conveniences of four years in Taft had made an imprint on them. Bessie was disappointed because she couldn't use her washer. We were always concerned about the kids, particularly Mickey and Phyllis. Heat was from a wood burning fireplace and burning kitchen stove. Lighting came from kerosene lanterns.

Mickey had been promised a puppy when we got there. We got him a rat terrier, the first of many small dogs. They did not do well in this climate. Bob had brought Pal, his German Shepherd, from Taft. Pal did not survive the dampness, soon catching distemper and dying. It was a sad day watching my boy walk up a hill carrying his dog and a shovel. He would make a 5" tall statue out of bronze which closely resembled Pal. I said before that he was good working with metal, and he did an excellent job on this project.

Mickey's puppy also died. Over time, he got a couple more dogs, but small dogs did not do well with us. I had six hounds that I used for rounding up sheep. They had no problems with the cold dampness of a northern California winter.

Two old gold seekers were panning gold in Bear River and in several creeks that ran through the ranch. They were also living in the cabin and didn't seem to be bothering anything. Bessie did not like them being there and told them to leave several times. They would leave for a few days and come right back. She even posted the cabin, but this only made them hide when they saw her Plymouth come around. I did nothing to discourage them and often talked with them. However, I always backed her when she was around.

One of the old fellows had a tumor on his face and lost an eye because of it. I felt sorry for him. Bessie had been raised to believe that people with handicaps were being punished by God for something they or their family had done. Outside of our own family, she had little compassion for the less fortunate. She was teaching this to the children and I hated to see that. I guess that being raised in a strict religious environment early in the 20th century had instilled these beliefs.

While in Taft, the family had always attended the Christian church, but finding none in Auburn, we found a Baptist church that seemed to hold the same beliefs that we did. We attended services on a regular basis.

Despite the fact that we were living in Nevada County, we were told that our children would attend school in Placer County. This meant the kids would walk about two blocks, cross the Bear River Bridge, and catch the bus at the Bear River Convenience Store.

At this time, Mickey was afraid of heights and, in the evenings, Bob would climb up to the top rail on the bridge and walk across the bridge on a six inch steel beam with a fifty feet drop into shallow rocky water. Mickey would get so scared by this that he could not walk. He would get in the middle of the road and crawl across the bridge. We did not know of this at the time, so nothing was done to stop it. Fortunately, Highway 49 had little traffic in those days.

I was keeping busy checking the fences and setting up a couple of corrals to keep the horses in. We were anxiously awaiting the arrival of horses and sheep. It was early November of 1940 when the horses arrived. I was glad to see them and the saddles.

One of the horses was named Muscalla and he was the meanest thing you have ever seen. The Indians had tried to talk me out of buying him. I had calmed him down and had ridden him, much to the surprise of the Indians. They told me that I was the only one who had ever stayed on him. This did not change during the time I had him. Even with me, I would have to go through a bucking session with him each and every time I got on him. I loved it and I believe he must have liked challenging me. I had bought a pony, primarily for Phyllis and Mickey, but found her to be an excellent cutting horse. I used her quite a bit. She was smart and gentle. Muscalla was always a challenge. The kids named the pony, "Penny", as there was a white spot shaped like a penny on her otherwise black head. They could ride her, either with or without a saddle and bridle.

I got a telegram from my dad that the sheep had been shipped. He had figured that it would save some shipping costs if they were sheared prior to loading. This was one of the mistakes made in this venture. We were paying by the carload, not by weight, and newly sheared sheep in cold, damp weather could turn into a problem. Of course, everyone from outside California thought the weather was always perfect.

From the day the sheep arrived, things kept getting worse. I had bought an old Ford stake body truck and this was the only means of transporting them to the ranch. They were placed in pens at the Roseville livestock yard and we were being charged for feed and the space they occupied.

By working day and night, we got them unloaded and into pastures in four days. The only help was Bob and two hired hands. I worked almost around the clock and the two hired hands worked days. Bob would work after school until late at night and even missed a couple of days at school trying to help. My partner mysteriously failed to put in an appearance during this ordeal. I doubt if he would have been much help anyway as he seemed quite disinterested when it came to work on the ranch.

The winters of 1940 and 1941 were two of the worst ever in northern California. The single fence around the main acreage meant that the sheep had roughly 1,500 acres to roam on. They went in small herds, going different directions. Texas had been much different because the land was semi-flat and the visibility was good. In the foothills that were heavy with pine trees, one had to listen for them rather than visually see them.

My son, Bob, was working his butt off and missing school. It was his senior year. We could have used Gordon, but he had chosen to remain working for the oil company in Taft. I guess he was the smart one. The two hired men were working long hours and were doing their best.

Bob got poison oak really bad. We got medication and salve from a doctor, but nothing seemed to help. One day, he spilled kerosene from a lantern on it. It quit itching and cleared up almost overnight. This became our standard medication for poison oak, which was abundant. No one else seemed to be bothered by it. Mickey rubbed some leaves on his arm hoping for sympathy, but all he got was two little marks that looked like mosquito bites.

My partner seemed to know when Bessie was fixing fried chicken, mashed potatoes, and gravy and would show up on those days. Other than that, he remained invisible.

Joan and Bessie were not getting along well and I stood up for Bessie. I realized later that we weren't being fair, but who says parenting is always fair? Bessie would not allow her to wear the clothes that were popular. The jitterbug was a popular dance and Bessie thought it was sinful. Joan had a Victrola record player on which she played records and occasionally danced with the door in her room. Bessie could not handle this. She often told the younger ones that they might grow up to be wicked and spiteful like their sister, Joan. I realized later that this was no way to treat a teenager, especially our own daughter. To her credit, Joan continued to be her own person, but I feel that she never forgave us.

Phyllis and Mickey were adapting well to the new surroundings. However, Mickey had been in kindergarten in Taft and this was not available in Auburn. Therefore, he was put into the first grade before his time and was the youngest in his class.

Near Auburn, there was an Indian reservation and the Indian kids attended the Auburn schools. Mickey's previous exposure to Indians was in western movies. He started staring at them, expecting them to attack at any time. One did, every day after school. First grade got out at 2:00 p.m. and the rest of the school at 3:00 p.m. The bus did not run until 3:20 p.m. So, Mickey had over an hour to run and hide or get beaten up. He began paying a bigger kid 15 cents a day, his lunch money, to hold the Indian boy while he ran and hid. Then he would come home starved. On the days when Bessie sent him with a bagged lunch, he would get beaten up.

I talked to him about this problem and told him that I thought if he hit this boy real hard in the face, that he would probably leave him alone. I don't know if it was a sucker punch or not, but Mickey came home quite proud the next day and the problem was over.

We had some sick sheep and were working hard at finding them and getting them away from the herd. Bessie was a great help. She fixed everyone breakfast, got the kids off to school, and brought us lunch every day. Dinner would be ready when we got home, even though it often had to be warmed up. It was often very late when we made it in.

I worried about her because all the roads on the ranch were dirt. There was a fairly high clay content so that they did not bottom out on you, but we were having a lot of rain and they were slick. There were several creeks to cross and none of them had bridges. They just had places where a car could make it through, if you could recognize the right spot.

One of the things that we all had in common was our work ethic. "Work hard, always be there, and be punctual. If you work for someone, do what they want you to do." I believe the children and most of the grandchildren inherited these traits. Believe me, it works!

Except for church, our social life was non-existent. The kids wanted to join the 4H Club and Bessie and I had inquired about joining the Farm Bureau. However, we did not have time to follow up on any of this until later.

Occasionally, you would meet someone at the small store and gas station located by the river. There was a bulletin board and it was generally just a friendly place to meet. The kids caught the bus at this spot.

One day I had stopped by the store to get some gasoline and met a well-dressed man. His name was Joe Arnsburg and he had a big house on the hill across the street, just above the store. He was a chiropractor and he practiced out of his residence. I never saw any cars or heard of any patients, so I figured that he must have money. It didn't appear that his practice was a profitable venture.

He invited me to bring the family to dinner on the following Saturday evening and I accepted. It would be good to meet someone and get out for a change.

Their house was large and very nice by 1940 standards. We had a very nice dinner. After dinner, the women and children went into the parlor and Joe and I went into his den and had a couple of drinks. He offered me a cigar, which I refused. Tobacco of any type was not my game.

He struck up a conversation, just chit chat. Then, he kind of shocked me by what came next. He said, "Jack, you know that you have a nice piece of land here and this country will grow. It would grow right here at the bridge if we had electricity. Currently, the people at the store and me have generators. No one else has any power for five miles either direction. I doubt if Pacific Gas and Electric (PG&E) gets power here for five years. Now, Jack, PG&E leaves reels of cable and poles laying all over the country side. In fact, I've got quite a collection in my back yard. There are a couple of guys who pick them up for me and bring them here. I pay them one dollar a reel and two dollars for poles delivered here. Now, I feel that some smart people could tap into existing lines a few miles away, run some underground cable for a short distance so as not to be obvious, then set poles and run lines to here. Then we could build a small substation and deliver power to whoever wanted it. It would be a long time before PG&E caught up with this and, when they did, they would be happy because things were already installed for them." The plan sounded great. We'd have ourselves a town and it would be named Gotchersville. It's funny how a few glasses of whiskey will develop plans. I never ran into Joe again. I later heard that he had been arrested for stealing poles and cable and selling it back to the electric company. Gotchersville was dead and the sheep were dying.

CHAPTER 16

THE FADING RAINBOW

Pneumonia hit the herd and I began rounding up those that weren't sick and taking them to the auction in Roseville. I brought in two or three trucks loaded with sheep and sold them. The total was about 70 sheep. Soon the sheep were dying as we rounded them up. Sheep are funny animals. If you get them into a corral and one lays down and dies, the rest are liable to lay down and die, too.

Meanwhile, the state agricultural people got wind of a sick herd and, all of a sudden, we had state inspectors putting up quarantine signs and guarding our gates. We were told to bury the dead sheep 10 to a hole and to pour 100 pounds of lye on them. We followed instructions, but we sure were digging a lot of holes.

We worked our tails off, but the herd was lost. We shut down our operation leaving only a few hardy strays in isolated areas. It was still rainy and cold and there were a lot of rainbows, but none ever seemed to touch the ground.

I had two things still going. We had some land that would be valuable and we had reemphasized Rule No. 8: Good judgment comes from experience and a lot of that comes from bad judgment. Amen!!!

We still had a little money saved and, wishing to save that, I went to work in a welding shop in Sacramento. We moved to a place closer to Auburn off Wolf Creek Road. It is now known as Joeger Road. It had three bedrooms with a cellar and electricity. It sat on 20 acres. There was a large barn on the land and a wooden fenced corral. I strung an electric fence covering about two cleared acres, but found the horses to be smarter than me, as this would not contain them.

The place was a nice size for me to ride Muscalla. Phyllis and Mickey could ride Penny within the fenced area and remain in sight.

Bob graduated from high school and I got him a 1932 Model A roadster. He seemed satisfied, but later on we learned that he was either deeply hurt or jealous because Gordon had gotten a new car for graduation. However, our financial status had changed since Gordon's graduation. Also, Gordon received his car for graduation from a junior college at the same age that Bob was when he graduated from high school.

In late May, I was offered a job at Boulder Dam. Bob went over with me and became a pretty good welder almost overnight. A couple of evenings with his dad and he passed his welding test. After a couple of months, Bechtel, the contractor I was working for, talked to me about going to Panama for a year. They made me a very attractive offer and told me I could bring anyone I wanted to work for me. Laborers would be Panamanian and all other positions would be filled by Americans. This appealed to me. I had a lot of family needing work and I needed some big money.

I got hold of cousins, Burl and Kenny Allison, my brothers, Fletch, Skinny, and Steve, plus Omie's husband, Lee. All agreed to come and work for me.

Once again, I packed those two old trunks and Bessie and the kids drove me to San Francisco to catch my ship. It was 140 miles of 2-lane road in those days. I tried to get Bessie to stay in a hotel in San Francisco that night, but there was no way she would spend four dollars for a hotel room when she could be home in three hours.

I found Panama to be like next door. It took us only eight days to get there and the ship stopped and stayed overnight at a couple of ports. Getting off the ship, I could see that Panama would be just as hot, but twice as humid, as Saudi.

I was met at the ship by J. H. Poloy, the Bechtel project sponsor. I had previously met him at Boulder Dam and he was a knowledgeable engineer with a good understanding of construction practices. We talked briefly and he said that the field was mine to run. I was to let him know what drawings and materials I needed and he would bust his tail to get them for me. It was obvious we would complement each other.

He explained to me that we were to run a reversible flow pipeline from one side of the canal to the other. There would be two pumping stations along this line. We would also need to do some repair work on the locks.

The priority was, of course, the pipeline. In case of war, we would be able to transfer oil products in either direction. Hitler was conquering Europe and the Japanese had overrun the Far East. We were staying out of it and I hoped we would.

Within two weeks of my arrival, all of my personal hires had arrived and the people Bechtel was sending us were filtering in. We were getting started and things looked like they would go quite well.

My son, Gordon, got hold of me wanting to make some big money. I arranged for him to come down and join us in August. I tried teaching him to weld, but his aptitude was not into welding, although he did barely pass the required test. I needed a timekeeper, a job that Gordon was well qualified to do. I made him and my brother, Steve, spend three evenings a week practicing welding. Steve got to where he could do a decent job of tacking. Gordon still needed a lot of practice. The men gave Steve the name of Scratch. This meant he was always dragging his welding rod rather than pushing the rod correctly.

It was nice having family there. Things were really good. We all had good jobs and were making good money. All of us had been very poor at one time and it was good that we had this opportunity to get ahead and enjoy doing it.

The other men outside of family were good, too. Most of them were either long time Bechtel employees or were known by Poloy. It was a lot different working with this bunch than with the British. These guys would be sober and could figure a way to do just about anything. The Brits always claimed they were specialists and could do only one thing. That is why we were able to hire them for about half of what we would pay an American. At least, there were no Brits on this job. Sadly, they were defending their country from Adolf Hitler.

We were able to furnish our own entertainment. Burl alone was a whole band. Fletch played the guitar, Skinny could play the fiddle, and I usually ended up on the harmonica. From our work crews, there were a couple more guitar players and a fellow who played a mean banjo. Lee and Kenny weren't particularly musically inclined. Of course, both of them had merely married into the family. They were not blood relatives. No wonder they lacked musical ability. Steve and Gordon joined them and the four of them would sometimes try to sing along. Talk about being off key! We did manage to have a few good, old fashioned, hoe downs.

In October, 1941, I had a chance to bring Bob down, so I sent the information home and requested that he be here in early December. On November 22nd, I received a telegram from Bessie that he had departed on the Kobe Maru and would arrive on December 1st. On that day, one of our men told me that they saw the Kobe Maru in port and Gordon and I went down to get him. We stopped by the customs and immigration office and they said no one had gotten off as yet. Gordon and I went over to the Kobe and boarded. A Japanese officer who spoke English was summoned. He told us that there were no passengers on board. I told him of my telegram advising me that my son was on board, but he said that they had made two stops along the way and that he must have gotten off. It didn't add up, but I returned to our construction office where I sat and thought a bit.

I always tried not to be prejudiced, but to be totally honest, I never really trusted Chinese or Japanese people. After thinking a bit, I went to the area where most of our men were working and gathered them up. I guess there were about 75 of us in all. We returned to the Kobe Maru. They had put a guard at the loading plank, but we totally ignored him. He wasn't about to make waves with so many of us. We boarded the ship and, once again, I met with the interpreter. He again denied having passengers. I told him that we were going to inspect the entire ship and he said he would have to get the Captain's permission. I assured him that, regardless, we would search the ship. He returned with the Captain and we used the interpreter to tell him what we wanted.

I believe the Captain understood English because, somehow, he remembered that there were four passengers below deck. Within a few minutes, Bob appeared with three other passengers. They were all happy to see us, but were unaware that anything was wrong.

Bob later told us that when they boarded ship, they were told to remain below deck for safety reasons and that the ship would make several stops. He said he knew it was close to arrival date, but he figured that this was just another stop.

We were fortunate that Bessie had sent the telegram and that Gordon and I went prowling around. Ordinarily, we just waited for immigration to get hold of us and say that we had a man waiting to be picked up at their office.

Having Bob with us made us kind of forget this incident until six days later when we learned that the Japanese bombed Pearl Harbor. We also learned that America had declared war on them.

We always wondered if this ship was aware of the coming war and had been told to bring some Americans home to Japan. This may have been the first pre-war incident.

Bob improved daily on his welding and, by the job's end, was the best and most productive welder I ever had. He would definitely let you know it, too. I needed him to cover for the lack of measurable productivity from Gordon and Steve. Actually they were productive, just not in the jobs they had been hired to do.

Bob was a welcome addition to our band. He had a good guitar that put out some fine sounds. However, he did insist on singing as a soloist from time to time. His welding was great, his guitar playing was very good, but his singing sucked. That may be the kind thing to say. He was quite a Bobby.

I really can't say enough about the people working for me, especially the family members. Everyone got along well. They worked hard and had fun doing it. I must credit Burl and Fletch for most of the pranks that went on. The welders did a tremendous job. We seldom had a repair and did not have to cut out any welds. We finished in June of 1942, almost two months ahead of schedule. By then, the country was at war and the need for this fuel line was urgent to the U. S.

Mr. Poloy asked what I would do next. I told him that I was going to look for opportunities in the northwest, particularly Alaska or Canada. He said he would probably form his own company and maybe see me some place.

Arriving in San Francisco, I took a taxi for the 140-mile ride from there to Auburn. It cost twenty dollars and Bessie had a fit. I could have sent a telegram, gotten a hotel room for two dollars, and she would have driven down the next day. We would probably have saved ten dollars.

Bessie had never told me, but after I went to Panama, Bot Tucker came around crying about his losses on the ranch. She thought it was our responsibility to repay him for his investment. She had signed over both the houses in Taft and had given him the Plymouth. I disagreed with her thinking as he had done no work, had not invested that much, and had stood a chance of getting rich if we had made it. We had more than a couple of go-a-rounds over this, but nothing would change. It was done.

I traded the Dodge in on a 1942 Chevrolet. This was the last model made for public sales during the war. Detroit had switched to making tanks and jeeps. I felt that we would be better off with a new car, as no one knew how long this war would last.

Bob and Gordon had come home a week before me. Bob had jumped into his Model A Ford and headed for New Mexico. A young gal he had met when we worked on Boulder Dam lived there. We were not surprised when we got pictures of him and his new bride, Louise, and their new car. He had traded the Model A in and got a 1939 LaSalle. The LaSalle was called a baby Cadillac back then. The LaSalle was built by the Cadillac Division of General Motors. I don't know if he was more proud of his wife or his car. Gordon drove to Taft and found his old job at Standard Oil.

Joan, Phyllis, and Mickey were doing well in school. Joan would be graduating the following year. She and Bessie continued to have their problems. Joan was going with a nice young man who lived down the road a short way. Bessie tried to forbid Joan to see him. This was difficult, as they rode on the same school bus and went to the same high school. Bessie's problem was that the boy's parents and grandparents were known to drink. Bessie did not realize how much this attitude was reminiscent of the way her mother had treated her. I shouldn't have just stood back. Maybe I could have done something to help them work it out. It never did. The mother/daughter relationship would never be of a close loving nature. I wish I could have changed that.

Just before my arrival, Bessie had made arrangements to lease the property across the road. It had 60 acres, a large house, a barn, and a detached garage apartment. This move was made necessary, as she had traded all the horses, but Penny, for 10 cows. The herd had grown to 40 and she was running a small dairy farm. She was selling milk, cream, eggs, fryers, ducks, geese, and turkeys to various outlets, mostly restaurants, in the Auburn area. Due to the war, she could not find a man to hire and help, so she hired a young lady who got free rent in the apartment and fifty dollars a month to milk and do a lot of the other chores.

The kids were doing chores. Joy helped with the milking, Phyllis with the housework, and Mickey took care of all the poultry, including the chore of gathering the eggs. He was very thin at eight years of age. Usually at feeding time, either the turkeys or geese would attack him and really beat on him. He had exactly the same problem that I had as a child. We had fun watching him sneak around, hoping that they wouldn't see him. He tried, but he seldom got away without being attacked.

With the war in full gear, meat and many other food and clothing items were rationed. Gasoline was rationed and Bessie was given coupons for four gallons a week, as farming was considered a vital operation. People living in town were given two gallons a week per car. Though gas was plentiful, the reason for rationing was that the Japanese had captured the rubber plantations in Indonesia. Therefore, tires were rationed and the quality of synthetic rubber in the U. S. was really bad. We would be okay for gasoline. Truckers had all the gas coupons they needed and they left some extras at the station where we traded. This station would always have some for their steady customers.

Tires would be a different matter. I managed to get five extra tires and I strapped them to the underside of the innersprings below the bed. It was a felony to be hoarding tires and, by doing this, they would not accidentally be seen.

Shoes for the kids were also a problem. I don't know how Bessie was able to keep the kids in them. No rubber was put in the shoes, so soles were a composition of mostly cardboard. Life expectancy for a pair of these shoes for an eight year old boy was about three weeks. Everyone was rationed to two pairs of shoes a year. Some styles of ladies shoes were exempt from this rule and Bessie would buy these for herself and have the extra coupons for the kids. War was not a time to worry about being stylish.

We had a lot of family fun while I was home. Penny was the only horse we had left. Phyllis and Mickey were pretty good riders. I spent hours in the corral sitting on the fence and having Mickey ride past me as fast as Penny would go. I would lasso him and pull him off. If I hit him high, I would just drop the rope. He loved this until Bessie spotted what we were doing and put a stop to it. She was worried about him getting hurt, and maybe rightfully so, but a cowboy would never understand.

Otherwise, we had a couple of family picnics and Phyllis, Mickey, and I would chase every rainbow that came up in the foothills of northern California. I was really enjoying this stay. I would get up early, do most of the chores, and realize how nice it was to be home. There just wasn't enough money being made for me to do this for a long period of time. We still had payments to make on the ranch and taxes were high on it. I scouted around some and was able to lease out a portion of it as summer range for some of the farmers in the valley. They still were having cattle drives up Highways 40 and 49.

After a couple of months, I took a job welding at the Mare Island shipyard. This was in Vallejo, California. My cousins, Omie and Lee, were living there and Lee was working nights so he could fish in the daytime. I stayed with them and went home every other weekend. Bessie and the kids would come down on alternate weekends.

One Friday, not long after I got there, I was called to the office. They told me I needed to go home at once. This was my weekend to go to Auburn and I figured that something was wrong there. I thought of leaving without changing and going straight home. However, I had gotten really dirty that day, so I swung by Omie's house.

Lee and Omie's house was where I was needed. Lee Albritton had gone fishing in the Carquinez Strait. This is an inlet with waters from the Pacific Ocean. Lee had climbed out on some rocks to get a deeper fishing hole and to get away from others fishing.

A big wave came up and washed him off the rocks. Lee had always been an excellent swimmer and he battled gamely. Someone threw a rope which he seemed to catch momentarily, but it slipped away and he was lost.

Omie, Bessie, and I spent the evening and most of the next couple of days at the spot where he was lost. We hoped and prayed he would come walking back. Lee was only 39.

Shortly after this, another crisis hit the Albrittons. Exa, their daughter, was going to get married. She was now 22, but had always been considered to be the wicked one. After all, when she was a senior in high school, she had been riding in a convertible that turned over. She was injured and had surgery on her right leg. This left a small scar for people to stare at and remember how wicked she was. Nice girls did not ride in convertibles in the late 1930's.

That was minor compared to what was about to be laid on the family. Exa was getting married to a Joe Finnerty. He was a painter by trade, but an Irish CATHOLIC by religion. That was bad enough, but Exa had decided to convert. Omie took it pretty well for a woman who was almost as biased as Bessie. Bessie really had a problem handling it. I attended the wedding without my wife.

I was keeping tabs on rumors of a job that the Corp of Engineers was beginning in Canada. It would be manned by available manpower and would be a mix of Army and civilian personnel. With the war on, there were not a lot of able bodied civilians around. I believe the cutoff for the draft was age 42. I was 44, so that kept me exempt. The only other exceptions were either physical exemptions or doing work necessary for the war effort. I decided that I would at least contact the Corp of Engineers, see what was going on, and what was available.

CHAPTER 17

NORTH TO THE YUKON

With the war in full swing, the U. S. and Canadian governments felt a vital need to build a highway between Dawson Creek, British Columbia, and Delta Junction, Alaska. It was to be known as the Alcan Highway. Fearing that the Japanese would eventually invade Alaska, a route needed to be established to move men and material. It was felt that the Japanese could successfully blockade entrance through the North Pacific. Along with the highway, there would be a pipeline and pump stations to furnish aviation fuel from Canada to Alaska.

I was hired to furnish crews to build a section of the pipeline form Dawson Creek to the Peace River, and then to build a bridge over the Peace River when materials became available. I would hire as many civilians as possible and the Army would furnish men for the shortfalls of manpower.

I immediately began sending telegrams to my relatives and to other good men who had worked for me in Panama and elsewhere. I ended up with about 40 men, which was sufficient for the work currently available. Many of my guys were young and able bodied and were looking for the exemption from Selective Service. As the job was critical, those working on it were exempt from the draft while working. My sons, Bob and Gordon, my brother, Steve, and about 20 others came to work there for that reason.

Edmonton, Alberta was the staging area for this 1,600 mile project. It was 371 miles from Edmonton to Dawson Creek where the project started.

The processing center was on the south side of the Saskatchewan River. The south side was a bit on the wild side, with sever bars and an abundance of hookers. There were a few warehouses and office buildings in the area.

Those coming to the project would process in Edmonton and be issued Arctic clothing. I am sure there were a few adventures by people coming to a cold climate for the first time, but the one I enjoyed best was the arrival of my brother, Fletch.

In those days, a man usually had a pair of good clothes and a set of work clothes. Fletch arrived in Edmonton in a shark skin suit, regular dress socks, and a pair of leather shoes. The leather was laced on the body of the shoes, leaving room for good circulation of air. This was what the well-dressed man would wear in Los Angeles with its almost perfect climate.

Edmonton was not Los Angeles, as Fletch would soon learn.

It was 50 degrees below zero when his train arrived. No one met him at the station, as he had directions from the train center to the process center.

At first, he didn't really feel the cold, so he decided to walk to the center. He almost froze in this short walk and made a hasty retreat back to the train station where a taxi was available. By the time he got to the center, it was too late for them to begin processing him or to issue his gear. They told him what hotel to stay in and sent him there with a driver. He could not go outside, but fortunately, the law of the north was in effect. Bars had to have hotels and restaurants which would be able to accommodate all the bar patrons should a bad storm trap them. So, he was able to eat and have a couple of drinks. He felt uncomfortable at the bar. Most of the customers were dressed in warm, grubby clothing and he had the Los Angeles clothing on. He went to bed early.

The following morning at 6:30 a.m., an Army jeep picked him up and took him to the process center. He went through his orientation on survival in the cold, signed a few papers, and was issued his cold weather clothing. The gloves and parka were extremely heavy, the boots were heavily insulated, and the pants were quite heavy. They told him he would not be leaving Edmonton for three days, so he was to just relax and enjoy the town.

He left the process center wearing his heavy clothes and felt comfortable out of doors for the first time since crossing the border. A Chinook came in within a few hours after he had his warm clothes. A Chinook is a warm cloud cover that comes out of nowhere and will change temperatures by as much as 100 degrees in a couple of hours. The temperatures had changed from minus 30 degrees to a more moderate plus 30 degrees.

All of a sudden, the Arctic gear was too warm and the clothes he had with him were going to be cold. He chose the Arctic clothing and would not change from them. Canadians sometimes go with tee shirts when temperatures climb so much. People were pointing and laughing at Fletch in the heavy clothing. I know he was enjoying the attention. He told this story many times and, though there were always changes, it was worth recalling.

Others arrived similarly dressed, but fortunately did not run into a Chinook when they got there. Of course, some had stories of getting rolled by the pretty ladies that hung around the bars on the south side of Edmonton.

The road was underway and it was quite an operation. There were places where there seemed to be no bottom. The Army had men cutting trees and filling these spots in, and often the trees were stacked six or eight deep, twenty feet across. Fill of this nature often ran a half mile or more. Then, you might get firm soil for variable distances before getting back to the swampy stuff, which was known as tundra. One didn't dare drive far off from where the highway was being built. Tundra could appear out of nowhere and bury your tires very deep.

Material was coming from wherever, whenever, yet progress was being made every day. One of my early responsibilities was to take the men and install two of the modularized pump stations and install the piping between them. The pump stations were generally about 60 miles apart and we would have about 10 days to get finished and move on to the next one. We must keep up with the highway.

We were looking forward to getting the pipe to the Peace River. At that point, my crew would cease to be pipefitters and would become bridge builders. The piping crews were getting 15 to 20 welds per day for each welder and they were good quality. It was obvious, with our manpower, we could not do six to eight miles per day. The Army furnished me with 20 welders. They would not be living in our camp, which was frustrating. We would start work at 6:00 a.m. and work until 10 p.m., or later. The Army guys would show up at 6:00 a.m. and leave by 7:00 p.m. I cannot say I blame them. They got paid no overtime and I am guessing that most of them made between 35 and 40 dollars per month in our Army.

For those of us who had worked in Panama, we found that the sometimes difference of 160 degrees between Panama and the Alcan Highway was not really all that comfortable. At least, there would not be any jock rash for us. Instead, there would be huge swarms of mosquitoes when the weather was above freezing. They weren't little guys, either.

Base camps had been set up at Dawson Creek, Peace River, and Whitehorse. Modularized camps would be set up and moved along as the work progressed. Army food was pretty good and, if the Quonset huts were not warm enough, we would be too tired at the end of the day to notice.

The Army bunch was doing a heck of a job on the road. They were making about eight miles per day. On the pipeline, we were only getting about six. We were told not to worry too much, that as soon as we got to Peace River, we would be building bridge and they would bring in others to place pipe. Still, we needed to and wanted to do our best. Americans were being killed by the Axis troops.

Once again, our entertainment was back to the musical talents of family members, and a few gamblers played poker. Every three months, those desiring it got three days off. Some of the men did not take this time off. Others went to Lake Louise or Banff in the Canadian Rockies. Realizing how far we were getting, we added a day travel time. Edmonton was farther and farther away, and it was the gateway to Lake Louise or Banff.

Men would try to have wives or girlfriends meet them there, but there were heavy wartime travel restrictions and some could not get clearance. Others would get bumped at the last minute. This made for some pretty unhappy campers who would take off from work, make the long trip, and find that they were alone. I had a couple of men quit when this happened. One was a young fellow and, the last I heard, he was seeing combat in Europe. He had been drafted as soon as his draft board was notified that he was no longer working with us.

My son, Bob, had brought his wife, Louise, up to Dawson Creek and, every chance he got, he spent time with her. This let them be together without a lot of travel. Due to the war, travel restrictions were in place. By keeping Louise with him, he would not have to go through the red tape of getting travel permits.

Meanwhile, my son, Gordon, began going to Lake Louise where he met a lovely young lady named Helen Banke. She was a Canadian gal from the Ontario area and was a waitress at the Chateau Louise.

Her name had been changed forever by none other than J. Edgar Hoover, head of the FBI. She waited on Mr. Hoover one evening and he apparently liked her personality, as did everyone. On a return visit, he asked for her again, but did not know her name. In frustration he said, "You know, the Topsy one." They finally figured out who he meant and she waited on him. From that point on, she would be known as Topsy.

By the second time Gordon went there, they decided it would work and they got married. When the tourist season ended at Lake Louise, she would join him in Peace River.

Meanwhile, letters from Bessie indicated that they were all well, but she was really busy. The herd had really grown and she was doing her part for the war effort by being a spotter. Volunteers, who were called spotters, would man towers used by the Forest Service looking for fires. These volunteers would be observing aircraft and would report and record a list of any aircraft that flew overhead.

The spotters were also looking for Japanese planes or balloons. The Japanese had sent a few balloons off and a couple of them, with incendiary devices aboard, had landed in Oregon. These caused small forest fires in Oregon.

Bessie had been hinting for some time that our silver wedding anniversary was coming up. She hinted that she wanted silver candleholders for this. Not being in an area where this type of thing was abundant, I told her to take the money she needed and to go buy them. I had figured that she would get some for about twentyfive dollars. Instead, she went to the best store in Sacramento at the time. It was a place called Weinstocks, and was similar to Say's of Fifth Avenue. Imagine my surprise when she wrote to tell me that they had just what she wanted and they were only one hundred ten dollars. Cowboys don't have very much sense when it doesn't concern saddles. I was never used to buying the finer worldly goods. I thought she could have been a bit more conservative, but she was my wife and I loved her. If that made her happy, then it was okay. After all, only a few months before, I had won thirteen hundred dollars from a guy playing poker. There was no way he was going to pay, so I let him give me his Rolex watch in lieu of the debt. Through the watch was only worth about four hundred dollars, accepting it beat not getting any of his debt paid.

Bessie was seemingly very tired in her letters and it had been almost a year since I had seen my youngest ones. I would definitely go home as soon as the bridge was finished.

We got started on the bridge and all was going well. The Army was barging a lot of material to us and other material was coming overland. The road from Dawson Creek, though crude, was passable.

The Peace River is a wide body of water. It has one of the fastest flow rates of any body of water in the world. On a stormy day, it was rough crossing it on a barge.

Gordon had Topsy with him and they rented a small cabin to live in. I often stayed overnight there to break the monotony of the camp life. I was glad Gordon had married. Before Topsy, he was doing a lot of gambling. Though he loved to gamble, it was not his long suit. She got him to only play in the lower stakes games and, as he was not living in the camp, he seldom played.

Most of our people were welders and metal workers. For a hobby, some worked on things like belt buckles, rings, and other jewelry items. Bob made a ring for me out of a silver spoon and a 1943 Canadian Victory nickel. The spoon was used for the band and the nickel was soldered to the top. I got many compliments on it. The ring, my saddle and lariat, my spurs, and my 30/40 Krag rifle were never far from me. Those were my main necessities.

I met some interesting people on the bridge project. One was a trucking contractor who often delivered supplies to us. We both liked to talk and I believe that he was purposely waiting for deliveries for us so we could sit and talk. He told me that he had left Saskatchewan with his wife and three daughters after two tornadoes collided over his farm and mowed his wheat like a giant lawnmower.

He then built a tent skid to pull behind a wagon, loaded all their possessions on the wagon and skid, and left with his wife and three young daughters. Their ages were 4, 3 and 2. It was in the neighborhood of 800 miles to their destination. They had thirty dollars for making a trip that would take two winters. They showed amazing courage in their travels. One of the winters, they spent nesting in an empty cabin they ran across.

I felt sad when the time came for us to say goodbye. We both promised to correspond, knowing that we probably wouldn't. I did often wonder about what became of him.

Work on the bridge went very well and, in the late fall of 1943, we were finished. They had two smaller bridges to build in Whitehorse and I would be supervisor over them. However, the materials were not there yet and it was good for everyone that we would have two to three months off. We were a happy bunch, except for a few guys knowing the draft might get them before we started up again.

Gordon was the first one called, but he was exempted because of his poor eyesight. Gordon decided to open a truck repair and welding shop in Bakersfield with one of his old school mates as a partner.

Bob and Louise went to Carlsbad, New Mexico, and this let Louise spend some time with her parents. She was barely 17 years old and had been gone for almost a year.

I had to stay at Peace River a couple of weeks after everyone else to submit documentation for the Corps of Engineers. Then I was off to California.

The night I got home, Bessie, Joan, and Mickey were there to greet me. After a lot of hugs and squeezes, I asked where my baby girl was. They said she was spending the night at a friend's house. It was the next ranch down the road from our place.

After relaxing a bit, I said that I'd go after Phyllis. She had always been a daddy's girl and would be disappointed if I did not come after her.

The place I went was about a half mile away. It had a long driveway, one that was almost two blocks long. The drive took all of five minutes. Though it was dark, Phyllis, her friend, and her friend's younger sister were out playing in the yard. I was only about halfway down the driveway when Phyllis came running out. She said she knew it was her daddy. I was so happy to see her.

I stopped at their house to tell them I was taking Phyllis with me. The girl Phyllis was visiting was a cute girl named Beverly Santos. I met the girl's father, Jack Santos, and his friend, Emmett Perkins. Nothing out of the ordinary happened, but I had bad feelings about these men right off the bat.

When I got home, I told Bessie and Phyllis, "Don't let the children go near those people. There is something going on and I don't think it is good." I was to learn some of it on my next visit to Auburn.

There were a few exceptions to the Selective Service rules regarding the draft. Age, disabilities, and jobs vital to the war effort were three of them. The fourth one was exemption due to serious criminal behavior. Santos and Perkins were still civilians due to their criminal records.

During the following week, I stopped in Auburn and inquired about these guys. The Placer County Sheriff's Department and the Auburn Police Force were made up of people who were 4F. This was the term used to mean people deferred from military service due to age or disability. They were definitely not courageous, athletic-type defenders of the law.

It seems that Santos and Perkins would rob jewelry stores in Auburn. They both had long criminal records. At times, there would be shootouts between them and the police, after which they would take off for home. They were sometimes pursued to the city limits and, occasionally to the edge of their property. The chase would be given up and a few days later, they would do it again. Most of the things they took were high in gold content. They had a smelter, so gold would be melted and sold elsewhere.

Santos and Perkins frequented a bar in lower Auburn known as the "Happy Hour". This taunted the police to some extent. No one would come in and arrest them and, after a few drinks, they would go commit a robbery. One day, the old lady who owned the place was tending bar and her little dog was on the other side of the bar. The dog started barking and Santos told her to shut the dog up. The next time the dog yelped, Santos pulled out a gun, shot, and killed the dog.

In later years, these two men robbed a store in Yreka, California, and killed the owner, his wife, and three children, stuffing the bodies in the trunk of their car. Later, they connected with a Los Angeles hooker named Barbara Graham and beat an old lady to death in a robbery attempt. After being caught, the three of them were sentenced to the California gas chamber at San Quentin prison. They were eventually executed. She was the last woman executed in California. A movie was made about the woman. It was titled, "I Want to Live" and was nominated for an academy award. The star of the movie was Susan Hayward.

I had brought the usual array of gifts making Joan, Phyllis, and Mickey happy. This time it was mostly fur. Red and silver fox stoles were brought for the kids and Bessie got a red fox coat. The furs had snaps on the feet so they could be buttoned around the neck. Of course, with that many, they seemed to be of no value. The furs would often be left lying around the yard after Mickey used some of them to play hunter.

Bessie had the herd up to about 50 milk cows and lots of poultry. I decided that she would work herself to death. Mickey and Phyllis were still too young to help. Joy had married the boy down the road. He left for the military and she had a new baby boy. Bessie had continued her work as a spotter looking for enemy planes. I think she really enjoyed this. It made her feel a part of the war effort and gave her a high vintage point in some beautiful California country. It was also an escape which everyone needs from time to time.

I decided that this was enough. I bought a house from some people on the outskirts of Lincoln, a small town in southern Placer County. It was sad buying from these people. Their son, Carl, had just been killed in action and they felt they needed to move away from their memories.

The house came with a garage apartment, chicken house, feed shed, and an unattached laundry room. There were 10 fenced acres, which would be plenty of pasture for Penny. The house had three bedrooms and enclosed back porch that Mickey used to make a fourth bedroom. It was high priced, three thousand five hundred dollars, but I wanted the best for my family.

An engineer I met had some pasture land about four miles east of Lincoln that I rented from him. I hired a couple of cowboys and we moved the herd and then had a field day. We dehorned and branded all the cows. Bessie was angry about this because the cows were all pretty tame and she thought it was a waste of time and money. She was probably right, but it was my chance to be a cowboy for a day. The following week, I took the cattle to the Roseville stockyards and they sold in the auction the following Saturday.

A service man's pay was not much, so Joy went to work for the local Ford dealer. He was doing mechanical work, a lot of it, as there hadn't been any new cars for a couple of years. He also had a used car lot that did a good business.

Bessie had begun doing substitute teaching and she started attending night school in Sacramento to get her degree. They were allowing her to teach on a provisional license, as many male teachers were off to war. There was a shortage of teachers.

One day, Mickey and I spotted a beautiful rainbow. We jumped in the Chevy and began the chase. We ended up about 10 miles away in the town of Penryn. We thought we had found it in a fruit orchard, but at the last minute, it moved away from us. It would have been great to share the pot of gold with my boy.

It was time for me to go back to Canada. The material was arriving in Whitehorse, the biggest town in the Yukon territories of Canada. Sadly, I said goodbye to my family and took off by train to Vancouver, British Columbia. This was the first leg in my trip to Whitehorse.

I was not going to need as many men on this job. My son, Bob, brothers Steve, Fletch, and Skinny, along with cousin, Burl, joined me. We had about 25 others to join us. The work went well, but was slow, due to material deliveries. We got ahead enough that we were taking off every other Sunday.

Everyone always got along well and the Sundays that we were off, we spent together. This gave us a chance for a couple of fun time adventures. The first involved a plan to go ice fishing.

The lakes were frozen over and people would drill holes in the ice. They would fish through these holes. The first time we tried, we never got all the way through the ice, but we almost froze to death trying. We talked to an old timer in Whitehorse and he told us the lake we had picked was too shallow and was frozen to the bottom. Fish could not survive there. He told us of a lake with plenty of fish, not far from where we stayed. He also suggested that we build a skid with a tent, or else wooden sides, and a roof. Then we should drag it out on the lake, get a wood or kerosene heater, and sit inside and fish. This sounded great to us Southerners. The old man even said that we should drill the holes the day before. The holes would not freeze much overnight and we could have more fishing time.

We did as we were told and, two weeks later, we were ready to move the skid out on the lake. We even put benches on the inside as part of the skid. This would allow us to sit down while fishing. Saturday afternoon, we dragged the skid out on the ice, put the heater inside, and left Burl and Fletcher to drill the holes with a hand auger that we borrowed in Whitehorse.

About four hours later, Burl and Fletch reported in that they were finished. There were 12 holes drilled and we could fish as soon as we got there. They returned the auger to the general store and we all anxiously waited for the next morning.

Several of us were out there at 5:00 a.m., and most of the others said they would be along later. Anxiously arriving at the skid, we noticed one little thing. They had drilled the holes along the outside walls, not the inside ones where we could sit with a warm fire and fish. We would have been mad if it hadn't been such a dumb thing to do. Instead, we laughed and laughed about it. We decided that we could push the skid to the left and then push it backwards a few feet. This would enable us to fish in half the holes. We tried pushing it by hand at first, but could not get it to budge. Burl and Fletch drove the truck back to camp and came back with a chain so we could drag it over. It worked, but it was only 50 percent effective because half the holes remained outside. Thanks, Burl and Fletch. This gave us a lot of laughs for the next few weeks.

I got a telegram that Joan's husband, Buddy, had been killed in an accident. His squadron was having a picnic near McCook,

Nebraska. They were at a spot where they often dove off a bank into a creek. Someone yelled that the last one in is a Jap. Buddy was the first to dive. A sandbar had moved in overnight and the water was only about two feet deep. He broke his neck and died two days later on Memorial Day, 1944. Joan was on a train trying to get to him, but did not get there in time. What a tragedy. She was only 18 and a widow. She had a baby just four months old. Bud was but 19, himself, and was a Sergeant. He was buried with military honors.

I sent my condolences, but there is so little you can do at a time like this. She decided to put his insurance money away for the boy when he was grown. Being a widow of a service man gave her the opportunity to get a priority civil service position at McClellan Air Base. She took the job and was delighted with it.

Her work was in an old hangar that had been converted to an open area office building. There had been several bathrooms before the remodeling, but they were all designed for men. They had left the urinals in the restrooms. On seeing a urinal for the first time, she went home and told her mother that it was such a nice place to work. They even had a place to wash and rinse your hair. She told that to several people before someone told her what they really were. I understand she was quite embarrassed.

The next Sunday we had off, the guys decided we would go into Whitehorse, have a few drinks, and play cards or dominos. This sounded like a relaxing way to spend the day. However, the quiet ended when we heard a couple of young gals, on their way to church, start screaming. We all ran out and there, on the wooden sidewalk of the main street in Whitehorse, was a brown bear. It looked like it weighed at least 450 pounds.

One of our guys yelled, "Get to the truck and get Jack's rifle!" I yelled, "Forget the rifle. Bring me my rope!" They came back with my 30/40 Krag and the lariat. The bear began moving toward the edge of town. I tried to stay close to him as he moved away. I then thought of my long passed cowboy days and threw a rope on him. I ran over to the bear and hog tied him to a fallen pine. No timer was used, so we didn't know if it was a world's record or not. Even with three legs tied, this bear could knock a switch out of your hand if you touched any part of his body. The kids who were downtown had a lot of fun with this for the next couple of hours. We then decided to take the bear into the woods and let him go.

This would be our last Sunday off work. Materials began to arrive and we were really busy for the next couple of months.

When we were 90 percent complete, I was asked to go to Nome, Alaska, for a couple of weeks to inspect some tank work. I left Fletcher in charge at Whitehorse and went to the coldest place I have ever been. Fortunately, I was only there for three weeks. The third or fourth day in Nome, my nose froze and I required some medical attention.

I got one letter from Bessie while in Nome. It was kind of a shocker. My mom had been up to visit her. She had brought her new husband. Knowing my mom, that was no great surprise. However, her new husband was one of her old ones, Odie Odum. He had been one of my stepfathers when I was just a boy. I hoped they would be happy. Mom would be 62 this year. I guess Odie was about five years older.

Upon finishing the work we had been assigned, I decided to go to Anchorage to see what type opportunities might be available there.

CHAPTER 18

ANCHORAGE: AN ABUNDANCE OF RAINBOWS

It was early fall, 1944, when I arrived in Anchorage. Alaska was still a territory and many felt it would never become a state. Territorial laws were much more lax and enforcement was almost nil. This meant that not a lot of questions were asked and people, though friendly, did not offer much information. It was said that almost half of the residences were hiding form the law outside the territory.

Because of the number of men in hiding, missing persons could not be declared dead for seven years. Even then, it took court action to declare them dead.

Anchorage was a real hustling, bustling city. It was the largest city in Alaska with over 4,000 residents. It was each meeting people. It seemed that everyone knew everyone by name and face, but no more.

Bars were open from 6:00 a.m. to 5:00 a.m. the next day. Everyone had to be out of the bar for an hour to allow owners time to clean up. This was a state law and was closely watched. However, that one hour probably led to more trouble than it was worth. A high percentage of Native Alaskans, the Indians and Eskimos, had serious drinking problems. During this hour break, most of the drunks would stand outside the bar fighting, yelling, and occasionally, knifing.

A few days after my arrival, I ran into L. J. Poloy, now owner of L. J. Poloy & Company. I had not seen nor heard of him since our days in Panama.

He said to me, "Jack, there is a world of opportunities here. Look around and, if you find something real good, let me know. I'll go in with you." I thanked him and we continued talking about various things. I was to run into him quite often over the next several months.

In the business opportunities of the Anchorage Times, there was an interesting ad: "Sawmill Company for Sale." I went to see the owner, an elderly man who seemed to be fed up with the business and wanted to retire.

After a little investigating and a long conversation with the mill foreman, I made a decision. The lumber business was for me. I envisioned Anchorage becoming a real boomtown when the war ended. Growing cities would need a lot of wood. Jack Gotcher would purchase the Alaska Sawmill Company.

Included with the Anchorage mill purchase was a saw mill in Seward, which is about 150 miles southeast of Anchorage. Though the mill in Seward was closed, it was in better condition than the one in Anchorage. Also, timber was much more plentiful in Seward.

Before the transaction was complete, I received an offer from a developer to purchase the Anchorage mill. His offer was more than I had paid for both mills. Talk about rainbows. I had made a profit before operations had even started.

Things were going well. I had an excellent manager at the Seward mill. He was very knowledgeable about the lumber business, from cutting the trees to the finished product. He was excellent on the paperwork involving inventory. My job would be to take orders, receive payments, and pay the bills.

Things were really going good, though I sure missed my family. I told Bessie to look into it and for them to come up, if possible.

Due to the war, travel restrictions were in effect. This meant that the War Department had to approve any travel by commercial transportation.

After a lot of filling out forms and waiting, we got the clearance for Bessie, Phyllis, and Mickey to join me. They would take the train from Los Angeles to Seattle. I did not understand that, as the same train stopped in Sacramento and took on passengers. But we were so happy to get approval that we didn't question their reasons. It was in the late fall of 1944 when the three of them boarded a Southern Pacific train in Los Angeles. Everyone on board was checked for travel permits. This delayed departure for about two hours.

Just before the train was ready to pull out, some military officials entered their compartment. Bessie was told that, due to military priorities, the travel authorizations had been cancelled. With nothing left to do, Bessie and the children boarded a Trailway bus back to Sacramento.

We were all broken hearted about the turn of events, but being patriotic Americans, we shrugged it off and reapplied. Hopefully, they would get approval to travel before Christmas which was only a couple of months away.

We felt lucky when our new request was approved in a very short time. However, once again after journeying to Los Angeles and boarding the train, the same thing happened again.

After this second heart breaking experience, Bessie and I decided to wait a while and see if travel restrictions were relaxed or, if by some miracle, the war would end. It was obvious that Mr. Hitler was going down in Europe, but the Japs were still being a pesky bunch. This kept Alaska on a state of alert. We had no idea when the war with Japan would end.

I met a bush pilot named Bud Thompson who began flying me to Seward once a week to look after the mill. Bud was in his late 30's and had been in Alaska for over 20 years. He never mentioned family and I sometimes wondered if he was on the run. We never discussed this, as the rule in Alaska was, "Don't ask."

We were both staying in the same hotel and enjoyed each other's company. We usually stopped in the hotel bar for a cool one in the evening and I told him of my desire to get into the cattle business. I told him that I had visions of a great population boom in Alaska when the war ended. I believed that if someone could raise cattle, they would get rich, very rich.

Bud seemed interested about it all, but most of our conversations were just kind of, "What if?" I would talk about ranching and he would talk about his airplane. He owned a Stinson Reliance, SR6, with a single engine. It was one of the finest airplanes in that era. Bud swore that they were the fines planes ever built.

One Sunday morning in February, Bud asked me to go on a pleasure flight with him. We flew just to see scenery and, flying out in the North Pacific, we circled Kodiak Island. We then landed to have a bite of breakfast.

After an Alaska-sized breakfast, Bud said, "Let's fly south and see what else is around." We flew over water for a while, then saw a few small islands. Bud swooped down over one and I saw a few heads of cattle. I told him, "I don't see why anyone would be raising cattle out here."

Circling a couple of times, we saw what appeared to be a Quonset hut, some radio antennas, and a smoothed out area which was obviously a landing strip. I think that we were somewhat confident when we saw an American flag. We were hoping it wasn't the Japanese trying to lure us in.

Upon landing, we were greeted by a Navy officer and two enlisted men. They said, "Welcome to Chirikof Island." They said they were there to gather and transmit weather data. They were also to watch for enemy planes or ships.

The officer's name was John Lowenberg. He told us that the island had been part of the seven million, two hundred thousand dollar purchase of Alaska from the Russians. That purchase was known as Seward's Folly. In 1850, no one though Alaska was worth anything.

There were several hundred heads of cattle on the island and a few wild horses. The animals were descendants of animals left by the Russians after the sale. The cattle were very wild and, on occasion, would chase Lowenberg or his men into the cold water of the North Pacific. They would have to work around some rocks and then run for the living quarters.

I had brought my rope and rifle and I proceeded to wander around the island. I came upon a mare grazing in a pasture and promptly threw a rope on her. I gave the mare a quick lesson in horse breaking, making a bridle by cutting out a piece of my lariat. I was riding her pretty well by the end of the day. I would bring a saddle and a bridle on our next trip. This way, the Navy guys could ride around without being attacked by the cattle.

During the afternoon, I shot a young steer and we had beef, broiled over a campfire for dinner. Surprisingly, the beef had not taken on a wild taste. Though not as tasty as domestic animals, it was good. If a person brought in some bulls to breed into the herd, it would be no time before the meat was grade A.

Lowenberg invited us to stay overnight and we graciously accepted. The sailors were happy to have some company. I believe that they were probably a bit tired of each other. Once a month, a small Navy boat dropped off supplies. Everyone enjoyed our chatter and, despite the absence of musical instruments, we even sang a bit. The radio played a few tunes we all knew, so we had background music.

The communications setup was quite elaborate. They had a large generator, transmitters, and some really super receivers. We were listening to a broadcast from Station KFBK, Sacramento, California. I was hearing a voice that my family might well be hearing. After all, they were living only 25 miles from Sacramento.

The following morning, they each gave us a list of things to bring to them on our next trip. Lowenberg advised us that the island got fogged in quite often, so we were advised to watch the weather reports before we flew in there blind. We assured him that we would be careful and would come back soon.

It was cool, but fairly clear, as we were taking off. At my suggestion, Bud circled the island a couple of times before we headed north for Anchorage. We were trying to make a fairly accurate count of the cattle and our estimate was that there were well over 1,000 head. There was a lot of high grass and brush on this small mountainous island.

After returning to Anchorage, I set out to find L. J. Poloy, but learned that he was in San Francisco and might not be back for a couple of weeks. I did some investigating with the Federal Land Authority on the status of Chirikof.

The island's previous owners had defaulted on a loan and the land could be purchased lock, stock, and barrel for the payment of back taxes and transfer fees. The total price came to just under fifteen thousand dollars. It wasn't a bad price for the land and the cattle. Now, if the rest of the cattle would prove to be the same as the one we had butchered, we were in business. With the sawmill turning a profit, this sounded like the Gotcher's had another money maker.

It was late March before either our work schedule or the weather allowed us to return to the island. This break allowed me to lots of leg work on what I anticipated to be a profitable venture. I checked with the bank and they said they would loan me ten thousand dollars, using the sawmill as collateral. L. J. Poloy told me to give him the entire picture and we would talk.

On our return to the island, the Navy guys were sure glad to see us. They hadn't seen anyone, except for a few Eskimos living on the south side of the island, since we left. The Navy had begun dropping mail and supplies from a plane, so their only contact with the outside world was by radio.

I had brought the sundry items they had requested and also picked up a saddle and bridle for them. I don't think they had dared to ride the horse. I guess the make shift bridle and riding bareback was not for them. They said that they had at least been feeding and leading the horse around. This would help in domesticating her.

They had butchered one more calf and enjoyed the steaks. They said they had left the remains on the ground overnight and a wolf was seen eating this the following morning. This put a slight scare into them, as they hadn't seen much wildlife on the island. Seriously, I doubt if they had ever wandered more than 100 yards from their compound due to the wild nature of the cows.

We went quite a way out to shoot another calf. I wondered if all the meat would be the same no matter where they were grazing. Once again, we had barbecued steaks for supper and again for breakfast. It was very good.

I took a little time and showed one of them how to cut up a calf so that the meat would not be wasted. They would have tastier cuts of beef, too.

The second evening, I revealed my plan to these guys. I told them, "If I am successful in buying the island, I plan to barge calves from Seattle, maybe as many as 500, and merge them with the herd. This would be done, not only to increase the size of the herd, but to eventually regenerate a tastier product."

I had checked with the Army about furnishing meat for the military in Alaska and was told to submit a bid on or before July 1, 1945. I would be considered along with any other bids. Some independent grocers in Anchorage had said they would be glad to purchase meat from me if it was competitively priced. We would now have a real plan to give to L. J.

On our return to Anchorage, I contacted L. J. Poloy. A meeting was set for the following day. After hearing my plan, a wide grin broke out on his face. He said, "Jack, this sounds like a hell of a deal. I know the construction management business. I know that everything I've ever seen you do in the past, you knew what you were doing and did it well. From the sound of this, there is risk, but there is also a chance to make some real big money. What do you need to start?" I went over the funding needed to file with GSA for getting to bid on the meat. I also covered what earnest money would be needed for the purchase of Chirikof Island, along with the estimated cost for purchasing calves and barging them from Seattle. Then, I told him of the finances that I had available to put into the venture. I was proud of the confidence he had in my ability to do all of this. I decided not to tell him about my venture of raising sheep in northern California. I may have told him of this in Panama. I didn't remember.

We left for his bank where he and I met with the bank manager. Before we left, L. J. had them issue a letter of credit which far exceeded our needs until we were selling meat.

CHAPTER 19

JACK: CATTLEMAN OR BUST

There were many things to do, but little time to do them. I wanted things in motion no later than the fourth quarter. The first setback came when I was informed that two other parties had indicated an interest in the island, so rather than let it go for the initial price, the sale would be awarded to the highest bidder. I submitted a bid for fourteen thousand, five hundred eighty-six dollars, which was one dollar more than the price that it was originally offered. After the bids closed, I was immediately notified that the other two parties had bid higher, but had not filed all the necessary paperwork. Therefore, they were disqualified. I had an island. Now, I needed a market for my cattle. I would still have to bid to furnish meat to the military, but I had until July 1st to come up with a number.

That bid would be fairly easy. I would have to bid on delivering one hundred thousand pounds of meat. There would be much more required, but this would be a unit measurement so that all bidding parties were on equal footing.

It was April 11, 1945. Bud flew me down to Seward to look over the logging operation. I had been neglecting this to some extent. Our foreman there, Bill Paquette, was a real pro. He had a lot of experience in the lumber business and needed little help or guidance in managing a productive mill. About all I needed to do was accept orders and payments and to pay the bills. Of course, of great importance was the task to see that the payroll got to the mill no later than noon on Friday. The business was generating a good cash flow.

I asked Bill if he needed to hire a few more men, as work had almost doubled in the last two months. He replied, "Jack, I have all the help I need. If work picks up more, I'll let you know. If it falls off, I'll lay off some." He was a good man with a good attitude.

We were just getting ready to board our plane when one of the guys in the airport came over to us to tell us that President Roosevelt had just died. A man named Harry Truman was taking his place. Like I had said before, I never voted for the man, but he sure turned the country around during the depression. I wish he could have at least seen the war end.

Bud and I flew to Seattle, by way of Homer, in late May and I made arrangements to purchase calves from a Montana rancher. The timing would be good, as we would need the cattle by October. That would be when he would be getting them to winter range, and there would be less expense at this time because they were rounded up.

I contacted a company that made barge deliveries to Anchorage. I was told that they could meet my needs if they had two weeks advance notice. This wouldn't be a problem. The company representative figured it would take about two and a half days from departure until the delivery on Chirikof.

In May, I got a letter from Bessie reminding me that Phyllis would become a teenager on May 31st. Time goes so fast. Had it really been 13 years since we lived in Borger? On June 10th, I would be 47 myself and Bessie would turn 47 on July 2nd. I stopped by the Post Office and mailed five dollars cash to Phyllis. I must remember to send Bessie something a little bit later. Otherwise, it might be as costly as the candleholders had been a couple of years before. Mail took about two weeks to reach home.

When I got my birthday card in early June, Bessie reminded me how old the kids were getting to be. Gordon would be 25 and Joan would be 20 in August. Bob, 23 in November. Phyllis had just turned 13, and Mickey was 10 back in January. I prayed that things would pan out so none of them would have to struggle like Bessie and I did. There had been some heartbreak, but also a lot of fun along the way. We had stayed together.

At this time, it seemed we were doing pretty well. The lumber company was making money and the cattle deal was really looking like it would be a big thing. If it turned out half as well as I dreamed, we would be very rich. We needed some praying and God on our side.

The first of July, I submitted the bid on the meat. Though I was not given the contract right off, I was told that I was low bidder and we would meet to finalize the deal around the first of August. They said that they probably would want to discuss my ability to deliver one hundred thousand pounds of meat by January 1st.

I was called in again to go over the land purchase and to give them some earnest money. With the help of L. J. Poloy, we seemed to be on solid financial footing. To my surprise, they told me that though I had no choice in the matter, I would be reimbursed for the continued military use of my island. I could live with that.

Bud and I had begun flying over to Chirikof twice a week to look at cattle pen locations. We needed to see what would be needed to land a larger plane and put the plan all together. Our sailor friends were always happy to see us. I had started bringing them some food items that the military did not necessarily drop down to them. We were really putting on the air miles. On July 18, 1945, I wrote the following letter to Bessie. (Letter not edited.)

July 18th, 1945

Dear Ones,

I hope you had a good birthday and that Omie was able to get up there to see you on it. did your teacher friends at the school do anything for it. well we are getting the island and the contract to furnish the meat so things are looking pretty good. Poloy has been a big help from the financial end. Of course he stands to make a big profit in this as well as us. How are the kids doing and is your arthritis any better. There is a lot of copper around here and I will send you a bracelet if you will wear it. I hope you haven't signed another contract with the school because before this year is out I think that we will be so well off that I won't let you work. if what I see is right we will be rich by years end and millionaires sometime next year or else I'll end out in the Pacific. Bud and I have been doing lots of flying back and forth. Lots of hugs and kisses to you and my babbyes. Love Dad

On July 22nd, Bud and I began to plan another trip to Seattle. In Seattle, I wanted to finalize the arrangements on the barges and also talk to the guy providing the cattle. Bud wanted to look around for a C-47, or a substantial aircraft, for hauling the meat from the island to the purchasers. He had heard he might be able to buy a C-47, in good condition, for fifty-four hundred dollars. That was a lot to spend, but we would have to do it to make money. Bud felt that, with the seats removed from a C-47, he could fly as much as 15 tons of meat to the mainland from the Chirikof.

We thought we would fly out to the island that afternoon for one last check on the runway. We needed some measurements so we could find out what work was necessary for landing a larger aircraft. We would have to get a piece of heavy equipment down there to do the runway and some other leveling work for us. I could probably rent a road grader, or a big bladed Cat, in Seattle for half the Anchorage price. We would be able to ship it up on one of the cattle barges and save a buck. We might even find a Seattle contractor to do the work.

Our Navy buddies were expecting us and had the fire going and the steaks cooking when we arrived. It must have been around 9:00 p.m. when we got there, but it was still daylight, as it was summertime and darkness is very short in the far north. We measured the runway around 10:00 p.m. with the assistance of our hosts.

The next morning, July 23rd, we woke with a lot of enthusiasm. Bud was extremely anxious to get back to Anchorage and get authorization for our flight to Seattle. He was sure that the plane he knew about would sell pretty fast. Though Bud and I had never signed any formal agreements, we had an understanding that he would be responsible for all transportation needs and would charge me a competitive rate.

We had breakfast with Lowenberg and told him that we were going back to Anchorage within the hour. He advised us against it. He said, "Jack, there is a fast moving storm coming out our way and you would be wiser to sit this one out. It should move away fairly fast."

After he told us that, Bud and I swung into action, as we were still intent on getting to Anchorage. We were airborne within the hour and were approaching Kodiak when the storm caught us. Kodiak air traffic control was reporting zero visibility. We asked for permission to land. They asked how much fuel we had and Bud told them he could fly about four more hours. They advised us to either go on to Anchorage and see if we could outrun the storm, or to circle the island a few times and see if the storm lifted. We chose to circle.

As we circled, I was thinking of the opportunities on the horizon and of my family. Also, there was a brief flashback to Rule Number 8 of the Cowboy's Creed: "Good judgement comes from experience and a lot of that experience comes from bad judgement."

I was praying that we had not used some of that bad judgement in our decision to leave Chirikof Island. We did not need a bad experience under these conditions.

What was really needed was a break in the clouds and that elusive rainbow peeking through.

A telegram was sent to Bessie the following day, which read:

WESTERN UNION

BESSIE GOTCHER   July 25, 1945
P. O. BOX 386
LINCOLN, CALIF

PHONE 303-M
THE PLANE CARRYING YOUR HUSBAND JACK GOTCHER
HAS NOT BEEN HEARD FROM AND IS OVER 24 HOURS
LATE IN ITS ARRIVAL AT ANCHORAGE. STOP. A SEARCH
HAS BEEN STARTED AND ALL EFFORTS TO LOCATE ARE
BEING TAKEN. STOP. WE WILL KEEP YOU ADVISED.
STOP.

ALBERT ELLIS
CAPTAIN
ALASKA TERRITORIAL POLICE
ANCHORAGE, ALASKA

The Gotcher family was devastated. Omie and her family drove to Lincoln from Vallejo. Gordon was living in the Bay Area and he and Topsy headed home. It was hard reaching Bob in Carlsbad, as he had no phone. He responded by phone the following day to the telegram he received. He and Louise were on their way. Fletcher and Grandma Lona drove up from Los Angeles after notification. Relatives and friends all over the country were notified.

Two days later, another telegram arrived:

WESTERN UNION

BESSIE GOTCHER   July 27, 1945
P. O. BOX 386
LINCOLN, CALIF

PHONE 303-M
NO NEW INFORMATION AT THIS TIME. STOP. ALL
FISHING CANNERIES IN THE AREA HAVE BEEN ASKED
TO LOOK FOR DEBREE. STOP. WE ARE CONTINUING
TO SEARCH. STOP. WILL ADVISE OF ANY NEW
DEVELOPMENTS. STOP.

ALBERT ELLIS
CAPTAIN
ALASKA TERRITORIAL POLICE
ANCHORAGE, ALASKA

Bob and Louise arrived from New Mexico and the family sat
and tried to make decisions as to what could be done. It was finally
decided that everyone would chip in and Gordon would fly to
Anchorage and see how the search was going. He would also look
after his father's interests. Gordon was only 25 years old and not
experienced in the tasks ahead, especially with the trauma that was
involved in the loss of his father. After receiving travel clearance from
the government, he departed on July 31st.

The FAA and Territorial Police assured Gordon that all was
being done that was possible, and that the search would continue.
On August 4th, they again gave reassurances that the search would
continue.

On August 6, 1945, the Enola Gay, a B-29 bombing aircraft, dropped an atomic bomb on Hiroshima, Japan. A few days later, another atomic bomb was dropped on Nagasaki. The Japanese surrendered and World War II was at an end.

Captain Ellis advised Gordon that the search would be abandoned. He felt that there was no longer hope.

Since he needed transportation, Gordon searched the logical places to find his dad's car. He then notified the police that it was missing. The 1942 Chevrolet was a highly sought for automobile since it was the latest model made prior to the war. Even with the help of the police, the car was never found.

After securing a lawyer to look after his father's interests, Gordon quickly learned about territorial laws. The seven-year law would be in effect. The lumber company would be placed in trust and, if Jack did not appear within that length of time, assets from the trust would go to the next of kin. This could be overcome, but it would be a costly endeavor. That decision would have to be made by Bessie.

Seeing that nothing more could be accomplished, Gordon gathered his father's personal effects and shipped them home. These included a trunk, a ½-oil barrel with a clamp-on lid. His clothing and personal effects were packed in this trunk. Sent separately were an old 30/40 Krag rifle and a Model 74 Winchester 22, with a hex barrel, manufactured in 1911.

The investment for the purchase of Chirikof was cancelled, as there was really no one with the knowledge to take over that type of project. It would remain in trust, even if operations continued.

After having done as much as he felt was possible, Gordon began the long, lonely trip home. Ironically, the plane he was on got caught in some fierce Pacific Ocean fog near Homer and was nearly lost.

Upon arriving at home, Gordon gave Bessie all available information. She readily accepted that Jack was gone and contacted the lawyer that Gordon had hired. She asked him to proceed with all efforts to claim and sell the lumber mill on her behalf. Her reasoning being, "Jack is gone and Phyllis and Mickey have to be raised, so I need the money now." The lawyer proceeded with this difficult assignment.

Gordon also accepted the loss of his father, though he had probably been the one closest to him. His attitude, which was a good one, was that life must go on.

Bob hung on to hope. He hoped that Jack land Bud might have decided to disappear. What the reasoning was behind that thinking is not known.

Why would they just disappear when the picture was so bright? Bob said that sometimes he would be driving down a highway and see a car headed in a different direction, being driven by a person who looked like his dad. He would sometimes turn around and try to follow the car, but with no luck. Bob loved to write songs and wrote one for his dad.

Joan, who always felt somewhat unloved, felt that he would not disappear on his own, due to his attachment to other family members.

Phyllis was sure he was lost forever. She loved him so much and she knew he could not leave her. It really hurt her. She had always felt that she was "Daddy's girl", and she probably was.

Mickey was 10 and could live a life of pretending for several years to come. He believed his dad was Robinson Crusoe and that he would come down off the mountain someday and tell of all his adventures. There was no proof or real reason for him to die, in Mickey's mind.

One of Bob's poems was not greatly written, but expressed his grief:

MISSING AND AWAY

A storm blew in one morning,
Over the island of Kodiak.
Caused a plane to miss the beacon
That was shining for our dad.

And when the storm was over,
A search was soon begun.
But no place in the Aleutians
Had wreckage on the sand.

When we see an airplane soaring,
We think of many things.
You strain your eyes to see the numbers
That are painted on the wings.

Your heart is in your throat
When you hear an engine roar.
You can't help but wonder
If you'll see your dad once more.

Now we know that he is flying,
Though he is missing and away.
'Cause the Lord takes care of people
Who are missing in a plane.

Now here's to a great man
Who kept the things he had,
The love of his family,
For a wonderful dad.

When his effects did arrive, they were placed in an outside laundry room about 50 feet from the house. Bessie went through them and pulled out a few personal effects to give to various family members. Then, she forbade Mickey and Phyllis to look at them again. Mickey liked to go in and touch things that had been his dad's. He saw nothing of value or anything that would be a source of embarrassment to his family. But, Bessie had said, "Hands off!" She caught him in there a short time later.

Bessie expressed her cruel side by whipping Mickey unmercifully with a willow switch. It could hardly be called a whipping. It was more like a beating. He had been looking in his dad's personal stuff which she had stored in the outside laundry shack. He had welts on his back that stayed there for several days. This was nothing new. She had beaten him several times before. Once, it was because she thought he had broken a jar of blackberry jam. She later learned that Phyllis was the guilty one, if an accident is guilt, but there were no apologies. In later years, she would have been jailed, but this was the 1940's.

However, Mickey continued to go through his dad's clothes and things whenever he could get back in the laundry room. There was a certain mystic about holding one of Jack's gloves or a torch striker. After all, for the time being, that was all he had of his father.

There were times he would be doing this and Bessie would come out in the back yard. Mickey would be very scared. At those time, he would pray, "Oh, Jesus, please don't let her catch me. I promise I will never ever sin again." He said that prayer more than once. I believe he feared her more than the wrath of the Lord.

When he grew a little older, the girls told him that when the stuff first came down from Alaska, Bessie found a letter and a couple of cards from a woman in New Mexico. No one ever knew what these were about, other than Bessie, but I guess she thought Mickey might find something else.

About two weeks after the personal things arrived, Bessie had the kids take them out to the trash area and wait for Louie Ruiz, the trash man, to pick them up. She stood there all the time until he had either trashed things, or put them in the cab to use and sell. Bessie told the kids, "He is gone and it is best we forget him." Phyllis and Mickey thought that this was sacrilegious of her. However, they had a few things, at least for a while. Mickey got the 30/40 Krag and some knives. Phyllis got a picture album.

During the next three or four years, Bessie would occasionally take Phyllis and Mickey to the ranch, where they would sometimes hear the bawling and cries of a few stray sheep. It was too bad they all couldn't have been hardy enough to survive that first winter. Going to the ranch made the kids feel a nearness to their dad. This was a place he loved so much. Could he be herding those sheep around on the mountains, riding on Muscalla?

However, business is business and Nevada irrigation taxes were seven hundred dollars a year. Not that any water was being used for irrigation, but merely because Bear River and a couple of creeks ran through the land. Seven hundred dollars is a lot of money for a school teacher to be paying. This was especially true for a teacher with a salary of sixteen hundred dollars a year, with two kids to provide for.

In 1947, she sold the land for ten dollars an acre. After paying off the ranch, she was left with three thousand, five hundred dollars. She took three hundred dollars and bought a 1934 Chevrolet sedan. The sedan was named Hesibah and, with her driving this rather large vehicle, it became the terror of Lincoln. People would say, "Look out, here comes Bessie." Actually it was a good buy in really good shape and, even in 1947, there were long waiting lists for new cars. Detroit was slow in retooling. It took a while to change from jeeps and tanks back to automobiles.

The lawyer in Anchorage finally got clearance to dispose of the mill and, although the value was in excess of twenty-five thousand dollars, Bessie got a check for ninety-six dollars. Legal fees had eaten things up. At least, there were no longer responsibilities in Alaska and the family knew what they had.......very little!

The Social Security Administration had denied benefits to the widow and children because it hadn't been proven that he was dead. I am sure it was very difficult tracking down employment records, as Jack had worked all over.

CHAPTER 20

THE MYSTERIES OF JACK
(and a little bit about the other Gotchers)

A few months after the disappearance, the mother of Bud Thompson, the pilot, called Bessie from Utah. She wanted to apologize on behalf of Bud, hoping we would not be bitter to her or to Bud. She was in her 80's and just wanted to share her grief, I believe. How could we be bitter? Hadn't she lost her son, also?

A fire destroyed the Gotcher home in 1948. Mickey used the enclosed porch for a bedroom and was asleep. He had seven boxes of shells for the 30/40 Krag, along with a couple of other guns. Shells were going off by the time he ran out the back door in only his underwear.

Other family members were playing cards in the front part of the house. They got out fully clothed. Tragically, most of the gifts and pictures, all memories of Jack, were destroyed in the fire. One picture album was saved by the heroic efforts of a volunteer fireman. The elephant tusks were so tarnished that they went in the trash, along with swords, knives, and the 30/40 rifle. It no longer had a stock and was bent into a circle.

In 1958, Social Security finally gave Bessie back benefits for the children. She got a lump sum payment. This would help her retirement in later years. She had continued to teach school and got her permanent license with her degree. She had majored in special education. She gave up her tenure in the Lincoln school system to return to Taft, as they were paying teachers almost fifty percent more. The Taft ISD had a lot of money that they received from the taxes on the oil developers.

In 1959, while working in Reno, Nevada, Mickey saw the name of a Mrs. Jack Gotcher in the city directory. He went to the neighborhood that was listed, but she was no longer living there. One of the neighbors said that he did not know for sure, but he thought she had lost her husband in an accident about 15 years earlier. This seemed too close to home, so he quit looking.

Joan was remarried and was raising two more sons. They were living in south Sacramento. One evening in 1962, her son Ron, age 11, answered the doorbell. A man asked where Joan was. Ron told him that she was at college. Ron then asked, "Who are you?" The man replied, "I'm your grandfather." He then turned and walked away, never to be seen again.

After getting a Master's degree in Psychology at Cal State University in Sacramento, Joan did some teaching at the university and worked in the California penal system. She and her husband, Richard, moved to Oregon in 1965. For some strange reason, they began receiving mail addressed to Jack Gotcher. None of it was personal mail. It was just fliers of different origins.

Gordon and Bob settled in the Sacramento area after brief overseas jobs. They both continued to work in the construction industry. Gordon, in supervision, and Bob, as the best damned welder you ever saw. You can believe this or not, but he would agree with me. Both had three sons. Gordon named his first born, Jack Gotcher. Bob named his first born, Larrie Jack, "Larry", Gotcher. Phyllis married into the Noyes family and named her second son, Jack Noyes.

Tragically and ironically, Gordon's wife, our Topsy lady, was killed in a plane crash on New Year's Day, 1965. A neighbor had gotten a plane for Christmas. He dropped by and invited them to go for a brief flight with him. Gordon stayed home to watch football. Topsy left with their two oldest boys and a visiting neighbor kid. The pilot and his brother, Topsy, and the neighbor kid, went on the first flight over Folsom Dam. There were only four seats on the Piper Apache, so the two Gotcher boys stayed on the ground to wait their turn. Another plane was in the area and, despite clear skies and the pilots being aware of each other, the planes collided and the Apache dropped straight down into the lake. After many searches, even one 12 years later when the lake had dried up due to drought, no trace of the plane was ever found. However, half of the body of the pilot's brother had surfaced initially, so there could be no doubt. Topsy would join Jack and Cousin Lee in the group of lost and not found.

In 1968, "Larry" Jack Gotcher, age 22, was killed in action in the Vietnam War. He was Jack's third grandson.

Bessie died in 1970, shortly before her 72nd birthday. During the years, she never learned anymore about Jack. She never remarried and, when her two brothers, Tom and Harrison, became destitute after years of work without Social Security or pensions, she took them in. Tom died in 1963 and Harrison, in 1968. When Gordon lost his wife in 1965, Bessie quit teaching and moved in with him. She helped him raise his sons until he remarried in 1970.

Over the years, Bessie mellowed a lot in regards to social changes. She did not retain her disdain for different religions or nationalities. Part of this change was necessary, as teaching school in California exposed her to much more than she had seen in Colorado, and elsewhere.

She had always been opposed to any type of gambling, but after retirement, she made many trips to Reno and Lake Tahoe and did a bit of betting. She always explained her love of the slot machines by saying, "I only play the nickel machines and isn't gambling if it's only for nickel."

Mickey did a lot of traveling and, through the years, he would play mind games. He would think, "What if dad was to come back?"

He would think of all the family and political news that he could share with his dad. He kept his dad alive in his mind, but began to let him fade out by figuring that by 1980, his dad would probably have died of old age, anyway.

CHAPTER 21

CLOSURE

The years were rapidly passing and it had long ago become obvious that there would never be a final closure. It became, or at least seemed, certain that the plan had gone down in the waters of the North Pacific. Long ago, any thought of pursuing finding it had vanished.

Then, in June of 1985, Gordon got a phone call from a friend in Texas. He had read a short article in USA TODAY. It merely said, "A plane found on Kodiak Island may solve a 40-year old mystery." Some wheels began to turn.

Gordon and Bob contacted the Alaska State Police who, along with the Federal Aviation Authority, were investigating the accident scene. They felt that the remains of two people found near the site of a smashed plane were Bud and Jack. A sliver of paper with the words, "Alaska Sawmill" and the name Gotcher was legible. Also, the name Gotcher was found in a readable slip in a moldy old wallet.

Photos of the relics of the crash were faxed to the Gotchers and they were able to identify the Rolex watch, the spurs, and the ring that Bob had made many years ago. There was also a well-weathered saddle and a lariat nearby. Surprisingly, there were no guns. It was not common for anyone to be unarmed in the territories.

A mystery arose when a bracelet with the name of John S. Lowenberg, USN, was found in Gotcher's jacket pocket. They had no knowledge of the sailors on Chirikof Island, so were wondering just who this man was. Could there be another body out there?

Some three weeks later, Lowenberg was contacted in Ames, Iowa. He had made the Navy a career and was now retired. He recalled walking to the plane in a futile attempt to get Jack and Bud to stay. At the last moment, he reached in to shake hands with Jack. Apparently, the bracelet fell off his arm and Jack picked it up after takeoff. Lowenberg recalled kicking every rock on the beach in search of the bracelet. He had totally forgotten about it over the years. At least, there was good news. There was not a third body.

All signs indicated that, in attempting to circle Kodiak, Bud got too low and crashed into the side of a mountain. There are areas of Kodiak Island that are only accessible about one month a year due to weather, mainly fog. It was in such an area, near Port Lions, Alaska, that the discovery of the plane was made.

Workers for the Department of Fish and Game were tagging young bears near the spot of the wreckage. They seemed to always find the young bear cubs in this area. They finished and departed without seeing the wreckage. One of them realized that their orange tranquilizer box had been left and spotted it on the ground. They landed to retrieve the box and, as they stepped out of the helicopter, they saw the wreckage. It was not pretty well covered with brush.

It was later determined that the bear cubs had used the rubber on the plane's tires for teething rings. Although the rubber had long been gone, this still seemed to be a meeting spot for the young animals who seemed to be creatures of habit without the teething ring.

Mysteriously, neither body seemed to have been touched by the wildlife in the area. Bud's remains were still in the pilot's seat in the plane. It appeared that Jack had been thrown about 20 feet in front of the plane. The general feeling was that neither man had survived the impact of the plane.

Returning to Anchorage, they reported their find to the Alaska State Police. In turn, the FAA was notified and both parties attempted to return to the area. It took almost four weeks before visibility got good enough to let them land there again.

If Gordon's friend in Texas had not seen the little article in the newspaper, we would probably have never known for sure that our dad had been found. Back in 1945, the Anchorage Times had misspelled the Gotcher name. They had published that Jack Gotcher was missing and that the search had been primarily about who would know the Gotcher fellow. They did run into some old timers who remembered him, but they had no idea where any family members could be contacted.

Finally, the State Police and FAA got there and recovered the remains and personal effects of the two men.

After the investigation, Jack's remains were cremated and flown to California. A memorial service was held in Sacramento. A small crypt was purchased and the urn, with the ashes, was interned in the same cemetery that Bessie, her son, Bob, her grandson, Larrie, and her brother Harrison James were buried.

The story was a hot item in several newspapers across the nation for three or four days before it died down. Gordon and Bob were in high glory getting interviews and being on local television. Even after the story had died down, Bob would call the news media and tell them he had some more news regarding the events. However, that quit working very quickly. They were just a couple of retired guys with nothing else to do. Regretfully, neither one even mentioned Joan nor Phyllis in their stories.

An aviation attorney came forward and spent considerable time trying to locate the insurance carrier. Bud was a licensed bush pilot and was required by territorial law to have at least a one million dollars liability policy. After 40 years, it was like looking for a needle in a haystack.

As far as we know, this was the longest aircraft mystery ever solved.

Anyway, the cowboy had come home.

CHAPTER 22

A VANISHING FAMILY

There are very few of Jack's family left. Phyllis and Joan live in the Roseville-Sacramento area. Joan is now 77 and gets around pretty well for her age. Both love and spend a lot of time with their grandchildren.

Bob retired from construction in 1973, due to lung problems. He swore it was from welding and not from the three to four packages of cigarettes smoked a day. He was a fine welder and a layout man and, even though training methods have improved, he would still be considered to be one of the best. Bob died in 1988, just a few days shy of his 66th birthday.

Gordon spent a lot of years as a construction supervisor and retired in 1983. He passed away in March of 1992, at the age of 71.

Mickey is now 66. He followed in his father's footsteps, working in the Middle East, South America, the Caribbean, Canada, and Alaska, plus serving in the armed services in Korea in 1953. He also worked in 23 of the United States. Starting as an apprentice pipefitter, he progressed into supervision, then on to upper management. He always surrounded himself with good people and had fun all the way. It was ironic that, when Mickey worked in Alaska in 1976 and 1977, half a dozen people working for him had worked for his father some 30 years earlier.

The finding of his father had a much greater emotional effect on Mickey than when he first came up missing. He had kept him alive and played the mind games for so many years. When they found Jack, all the pretend games went right out the tube. His dad had been dead all the time.

All Jack's sisters and brothers are dead now. Les was still the reigning champion of square dance calling when he died. Steve, who seemed so lazy while working for Jack, made several inventions in the line of welding tips. The Lockheed and Douglas Aircraft companies gave him contracts to furnish new tips and to repair others. He became a multi-millionaire and didn't even have to get dirty.

Herb Needles, the man he conversed with so often around Dawson Creek and Whitehorse, wrote a book entitled, "The Dirty Thirties". Mickey was fortunate enough to meet and work with his son-in-law in the early 80's near Edmonton, Canada.

The 500 acres of land in Carmichael, California, that Jack could have purchased for forty dollars an acre is now a thriving community. It is the site of the California State Governor's mansion. The land values are very high.

The ranch between Auburn and Grass Valley became a weekend getaway for the rich and famous of Silicon Valley. What Jack paid nine dollars an acre for now sells for almost one hundred thousand dollars an acre.

H. J. Poloy, a fictitious name, became a large contractor and was a prime contractor in the building of missile bases in the late 50's and early 60's. He was the brother-in-law of a man who became a U. S. president. This may explain some of his success.

Little information was available for the time between 1907 and 1918. It is known that Jack lived with, and worked for, a pair of teamsters in the early part of these years. This was followed by employment at the King Ranch. A foreman, or a section head, befriended Jack and helped him with ranch duties and getting started in rodeos. Burl did some entertaining during his brief visit to Kingsville.

Jack chased the rainbows all the way, but he had good vision of what could happen and bad luck on what did happen. He came into the world with nothing and still had most of it when he left.

Times were very hard in that era and some men stand taller than others.

Our dad was a Giant!

We Love You, Dad!!

Printed in the United States
By Bookmasters